Y0-ATL-286

THE WORKS OF

JOHN GALSWORTHY

FICTION

VILLA RUBEIN: AND OTHER STORIES
THE ISLAND PHARISEES
THE MAN OF PROPERTY
THE COUNTRY HOUSE
FRATERNITY
THE PATRICIAN
THE DARK FLOWER
THE FREELANDS
BEYOND
FIVE TALES
SAINT'S PROGRESS
TATTERDEMALION
IN CHANCERY
TO LET

THE FORSYTE SAGA

STUDIES

A COMMENTARY
A MOTLEY
THE INN OF TRANQUILLITY
THE LITTLE MAN
A SHEAF
ANOTHER SHEAF
ADDRESSES IN AMERICA, 1919

POEMS

MOODS, SONGS AND DOGGERELS

MEMORIES (Illustrated)
AWAKENING (Illustrated)

PLAYS

First Series:	The Silver Box Joy Strife
Second Series:	The Eldest Son The Little Dream Justice
Third Series:	The Fugitive The Pigeon The Mob
Fourth Series:	A Bit o' Love Foundations The Skin Game
Fifth Series:	A Family Man Loyalties Windows

SIX SHORT PLAYS

PLAYS

FIFTH SERIES

BY

JOHN GALSWORTHY

PLAYS

FIFTH SERIES

A FAMILY MAN
LOYALTIES
WINDOWS

BY

JOHN GALSWORTHY

NEW YORK
CHARLES SCRIBNER'S SONS
1923

Printed in the United States of America

To

THOMAS BLAIR REYNOLDS

A FAMILY MAN

IN THREE ACTS

CAST OF ORIGINAL PRODUCTION

AT THE COMEDY THEATRE, LONDON,
On *May* 1921

JOHN BUILDER	Norman M'Kinnel
JULIA	Mary Barton
ATHENE	Sibell Archdale
MAUD	Agatha Kentish
RALPH BUILDER	Arthur Burne
GUY HERRINGHAME	Francis Lister
ANNIE	Olive Walter
CAMILLE	Auriol Lee
TOPPING	D. A. Clarke Smith
THE MAYOR	Laurence Hanray
HARRIS	Eric Lugg
FRANCIS CHANTREY	John Howell
MOON	Eugene Leahy
MARTIN	Julian D'Albie
A JOURNALIST	Reginald Bach

CHARACTERS

JOHN BUILDER	Of the firm of Builder & Builder
JULIA	His Wife
ATHENE	His elder Daughter
MAUD	His younger Daughter
RALPH BUILDER	His Brother, and Partner
GUY HERRINGHAME	A Flying Man
ANNIE	A Young Person in Blue
CAMILLE	Mrs. Builder's French Maid
TOPPING	Builder's Manservant
THE MAYOR	Of Breconridge
HARRIS	His Secretary
FRANCIS CHANTREY	J.P.
MOON	A Constable
MARTIN	A Police Sergeant
A JOURNALIST	From *The Comet*

THE FIGURE OF A POACHER

THE VOICES AND FACES OF SMALL BOYS

The action passes in the town of Breconridge, in the Midlands.

ACT I.

SCENE I. BUILDER'S *Study. After breakfast.*

SCENE II. A Studio.

ACT II. BUILDER'S *Study. Lunch time.*

ACT III.

SCENE I. THE MAYOR'S *Study.* 10 A.M. *the following day.*

SCENE II. BUILDER'S *Study. The same. Noon.*

SCENE III. BUILDER'S *Study. The same. Evening.*

ACT I

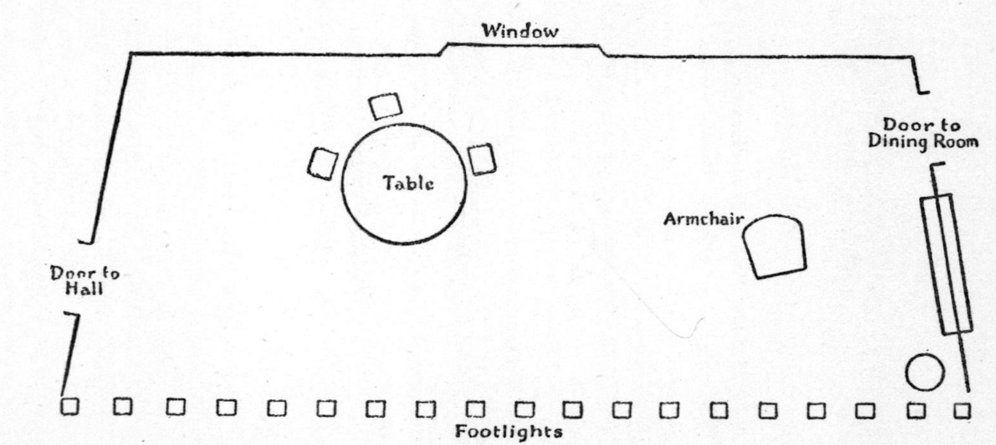
Window
Table
Armchair
Door to
Dining Room
Door to
Hall
Footlights

ACT I

SCENE I

The study of JOHN BUILDER *in the provincial town of Breconridge. A panelled room wherein nothing is ever studied, except perhaps* BUILDER'S *face in the mirror over the fireplace. It is, however, comfortable, and has large leather chairs and a writing table in the centre, on which is a typewriter, and many papers. At the back is a large window with French outside shutters, overlooking the street, for the house is an old one, built in an age when the homes of doctors, lawyers and so forth were part of a provincial town, and not yet suburban. There are two or three fine old prints on the walls, Right and Left; and a fine old fireplace, Left, with a fender on which one can sit. A door, Left back, leads into the dining-room, and a door, Right forward, into the hall.*

JOHN BUILDER *is sitting in his after-breakfast chair before the fire with* The Times *in his hands. He has breakfasted well, and is in that condition of first-pipe serenity in which the affairs of the nation seem almost bearable. He is a tallish, square, personable man of forty-seven, with a well-coloured, jowly, fullish face, marked under the eyes, which have very small pupils and a good deal of light in them. His bearing has force and importance, as of a man accustomed to rising and ownerships, sure in his opinions, and not lacking in geniality when things go his way. Essentially a Midlander. His wife, a woman of forty-one, of ivory tint, with a thin, trim figure and a face so strangely composed as to be almost like a mask (essentially from Jersey) is putting a nib into a pen-holder, and filling an ink-pot at the writing-table.*

As the curtain rises CAMILLE *enters with a rather broken-down cardboard box containing flowers. She is a young woman with a good figure, a pale face, the warm brown eyes and complete poise of a Frenchwoman. She takes the box to* MRS. BUILDER.

MRS. BUILDER. The blue vase, please, Camille.

CAMILLE *fetches a vase.* MRS. BUILDER *puts the flowers into the vase.* CAMILLE *gathers up the débris; and with a glance at* BUILDER *goes out.*

BUILDER. Glorious October! I ought to have a damned good day's shooting with Chantrey to-morrow.

MRS. BUILDER. [*Arranging the flowers*] Aren't you going to the office this morning?

BUILDER. Well, no, I was going to take a couple of days off. If you feel at the top of your form, take a rest—then you go on feeling at the top. [*He looks at her, as if calculating*] What do you say to looking up Athene?

MRS. BUILDER. [*Palpably astonished*] Athene? But you said you'd done with her?

BUILDER. [*Smiling*] Six weeks ago; but, dash it, one can't have done with one's own daughter. That's the weakness of an Englishman; he can't keep up his resentments. In a town like this it doesn't do to have her living by herself. One of these days it'll get out we've had a row. That wouldn't do me any good.

MRS. BUILDER. I see.

BUILDER. Besides, I miss her. Maud's so self-absorbed. It makes a big hole in the family, Julia. You've got her address, haven't you?

MRS. BUILDER. Yes. [*Very still*] But do you think it's dignified, John?

BUILDER. [*Genially*] Oh, hang dignity! I rather pride myself on knowing when to stand on my dignity and when to sit on it. If she's still crazy about Art, she can live at home, and go out to study.

MRS. BUILDER. Her craze was for liberty.

BUILDER. A few weeks' discomfort soon cures that. She can't live on her pittance. She'll have found that out by now. Get your things on and come with me at twelve o'clock.

MRS. BUILDER. I think you'll regret it. She'll refuse.

BUILDER. Not if I'm nice to her. A child could play with me to-day. Shall I tell you a secret, Julia?

MRS. BUILDER. It would be pleasant for a change.

BUILDER. The Mayor's coming round at eleven, and I know perfectly well what he's coming for.

MRS. BUILDER. Well?

BUILDER. I'm to be nominated for Mayor next month. Harris tipped me the wink at the last Council meeting. Not so bad at forty-seven—h'm? I can make a thundering good Mayor. I can do things for this town that nobody else can.

MRS. BUILDER. Now I understand about Athene.

BUILDER [*Good-humouredly*] Well, it's partly that. But [*more seriously*] it's more the feeling I get that I'm not doing my duty by her. Goodness knows whom she may be picking up with! Artists are a loose lot. And young people in these days are the limit. I quite believe in moving with the times, but one's either born a Conservative, or one isn't. So you be ready at twelve, see. By the way, that French maid of yours, Julia——

MRS. BUILDER. What about her?

BUILDER. Is she—er—is she all right? We don't want any trouble with Topping.

MRS. BUILDER. There will be none with—Topping.

[*She opens the door Left.*

BUILDER. I don't know; she strikes me as—very French.

[MRS. BUILDER *smiles and passes out.*

BUILDER *fills his second pipe. He is just taking up the paper again when the door from the hall is opened, and the manservant* TOPPING, *dried, dark, sub-humorous, in a black cut-away, announces:*

TOPPING. The Mayor, sir, and Mr. Harris!

THE MAYOR *of Breconridge enters. He is clean-shaven, red-faced, light-eyed, about sixty, shrewd, poll-parroty, naturally jovial, dressed with the indefinable wrongness of a burgher; he is followed by his Secretary* HARRIS, *a man all eyes and cleverness.*

[TOPPING *retires.*

BUILDER. [*Rising*] Hallo, Mayor! What brings you so early? Glad to see you. Morning, Harris!

MAYOR. Morning, Builder, morning.

HARRIS. Good-morning, sir.

BUILDER. Sit down—sit down! Have a cigar!

The MAYOR *takes a cigar,* HARRIS *a cigarette from his own case.*

BUILDER. Well, Mayor, what's gone wrong with the works?

[*He and* HARRIS *exchange a look.*

MAYOR. [*With his first puff*] After you left the Council the other day, Builder, we came to a decision.

BUILDER. Deuce you did! Shall I agree with it?

MAYOR. We shall see. We want to nominate you for Mayor. You willin' to stand?

BUILDER. [*Stolid*] That requires consideration.

MAYOR. The only alternative is Chantrey; but he's a light weight, and rather too much County. What's your objection?

BUILDER. It's a bit unexpected, Mayor. [*Looks at* HARRIS] Am I the right man? Following you, you know. I'm shooting with Chantrey to-morrow. What does he feel about it?

MAYOR. What do you say, 'Arris?

HARRIS. Mr. Chantrey's a public school and University man, sir; he's not what I call ambitious.

BUILDER. Nor am I, Harris.

HARRIS. No, sir; of course you've a high sense of duty. Mr. Chantrey's rather dilettante.

MAYOR. We want a solid man.

BUILDER. I'm very busy, you know, Mayor.

MAYOR. But you've got all the qualifications—big business, family man, live in the town, church-goer, experience on the Council and the Bench. Better say "yes," Builder.

BUILDER. It's a lot of extra work. I don't take things up lightly.

MAYOR. Dangerous times, these. Authority questioned all over the place. We want a man that feels his responsibilities, and we think we've got him in you.

BUILDER. Very good of you, Mayor. I don't know, I'm sure. I must think of the good of the town.

HARRIS. I shouldn't worry about that, sir.

MAYOR. The name John Builder carries weight. You're looked up to as a man who can manage his own affairs. Madam and the young ladies well?

BUILDER. First-rate.

MAYOR. [*Rises*] That's right. Well, if you'd like to talk it over with Chantrey to-morrow. With all this extremism, we want a man of principle and common sense.

HARRIS. We want a man that'll grasp the nettle, sir—and that's you.

BUILDER. H'm! I've got a temper, you know.

MAYOR. [*Chuckling*] We do—we do! You'll say "yes," I see. No false modesty! Come along, 'Arris, we must go.

BUILDER. Well, Mayor, I'll think it over, and let you have an answer. You know my faults, and you know my qualities, such as they are. I'm just a plain Englishman.

MAYOR. We don't want anything better than that. I always say the great point about an Englishman is that he's got bottom; you may knock him off his pins, but you find him on 'em again before you can say "Jack Robinson." He may have his moments of aberration, but he's a sticker. Morning, Builder, morning! Hope you'll say "yes."

He shakes hands and goes out, followed by HARRIS.

When the door is closed BUILDER *stands a moment quite still with a gratified smile on his face; then turns and scrutinises himself in the glass over the hearth. While he is doing so the door from the dining-room is opened quietly and* CAMILLE *comes in.* BUILDER, *suddenly seeing her reflected in the mirror, turns.*

BUILDER. What is it, Camille?

CAMILLE. Madame send me for a letter she say you have, Monsieur, from the dyer and cleaner, with a bill.

BUILDER. [*Feeling in his pockets*] Yes—no. It's on the table.

[CAMILLE *goes to the writing-table and looks.*

That blue thing.

CAMILLE. [*Taking it up*] Non, Monsieur, this is from the gas.

BUILDER. Oh! Ah!

He moves up to the table and turns over papers. CAMILLE *stands motionless close by with her eyes fixed on him.*

Here it is! [*He looks up, sees her looking at him, drops his own gaze, and hands her the letter. Their hands touch. Putting his hands in his pockets*] What made you come to England?

CAMILLE. [*Demure*] It is better pay, Monsieur, and [*With a smile*] the English are so amiable.

BUILDER. Deuce they are! They haven't got that reputation.

CAMILLE. Oh! I admire Englishmen. They are so strong and kind.

BUILDER. [*Bluffly flattered*] H'm! We've no manners.

CAMILLE. The Frenchman is more polite, but not in the 'eart.

BUILDER. Yes. I suppose we're pretty sound at heart.

CAMILLE. And the Englishman have his life in the family—the Frenchman have his life outside.

BUILDER. [*With discomfort*] H'm!

CAMILLE. [*With a look*] Too mooch in the family—like a rabbit in a 'utch.

BUILDER. Oh! So that's your view of us!

[*His eyes rest on her, attracted but resentful.*

CAMILLE. Pardon, Monsieur, my tongue run away with me.

BUILDER. [*Half conscious of being led on*] Are you from Paris?

CAMILLE. [*Clasping her hands*] Yes. What a town for pleasure—Paris!

BUILDER. I suppose so. Loose place, Paris.

CAMILLE. Loose? What is that, Monsieur?

BUILDER. The opposite of strict.

CAMILLE. Strict! Oh! certainly we like life, we other French. It is not like England. I take this to Madame, Monsieur. [*She turns as if to go*] Excuse me.

BUILDER. I thought you Frenchwomen all married young.

CAMILLE. I 'ave been married; my 'usband did die —*en Afrique.*

BUILDER. You wear no ring.

CAMILLE. [*Smiling*] I prefare to be mademoiselle, Monsieur.

BUILDER. [*Dubiously*] Well, it's all the same to us. [*He takes a letter up from the table*] You might take this to Mrs. Builder too. [*Again their fingers touch, and there is a suspicion of encounter between their eyes.*]

[CAMILLE *goes out.*

BUILDER. [*Turning to his chair*] Don't know about that woman—she's a tantalizer.

He compresses his lips, and is settling back into his chair, when the door from the hall is opened and his daughter MAUD *comes in; a pretty girl, rather pale, with fine eyes. Though her face has a determined cast her manner at this moment is by no means decisive. She has a letter in her hand, and advances rather as if she were stalking her father, who, after a "Hallo, Maud!" has begun to read his paper.*

MAUD. [*Getting as far as the table*] Father.

BUILDER. [*Not lowering the paper*] Well? I know that tone. What do *you* want—money?

MAUD. I always want money, of course; but—but——

BUILDER. [*Pulling out a note—abstractedly*] Here's five pounds for you.

MAUD, *advancing, takes it, then seems to find what she has come for more on her chest than ever.*

BUILDER. [*Unconscious*] Will you take a letter for me?

MAUD *sits down Left of table and prepares to take down the letter.*

[*Dictating*] "Dear Mr. Mayor,—Referring to your call this morning, I have—er—given the matter very careful consideration, and though somewhat reluctant——"

MAUD. Are you really reluctant, father?

BUILDER. Go on—"To assume greater responsibilities, I feel it my duty to come forward in accordance with your wish. The—er—honour is one of which I hardly feel myself worthy, but you may rest assured——"

MAUD. Worthy. But you do, you know.

BUILDER. Look here! Are you trying to get a rise

out of me?—because you won't succeed this morning.

MAUD. I thought you were trying to get one out of me.

BUILDER. Well, how would *you* express it?

MAUD. "I know I'm the best man for the place, and so do you——"

BUILDER. The disrespect of you young people is something extraordinary. And that reminds me: where do you go every evening now after tea?

MAUD. I—I don't know.

BUILDER. Come now, that won't do—you're never in the house from six to seven.

MAUD. Well! It has to do with my education.

BUILDER. Why, you finished that two years ago!

MAUD. Well, call it a hobby, if you like, then, father.

She takes up the letter she brought in and seems on the point of broaching it.

BUILDER. Hobby? Well, what is it?

MAUD. I don't want to irritate you, father.

BUILDER. You can't irritate me more than by having secrets. See what that led to in your sister's case. And, by the way, I'm going to put an end to that this morning. You'll be glad to have her back, won't you?

MAUD. [*Startled*] What!

BUILDER. Your mother and I are going round to Athene at twelve o'clock. I shall make it up with her. She must come back here.

MAUD. [*Aghast, but hiding it*] Oh! It's—it's no good, father. She won't.

BUILDER. We shall see that. I've quite got over my tantrum, and I expect she has.

MAUD. [*Earnestly*] Father! I do really assure you she won't; it's only wasting your time, and making you eat humble pie.

BUILDER. Well, I can eat a good deal this morning. It's all nonsense! A family's a family.

MAUD. [*More and more disturbed, but hiding it*] Father, if I were you, I wouldn't—really! It's not—dignified.

BUILDER. You can leave me to judge of that. It's not dignified for the Mayor of this town to have an unmarried daughter as young as Athene living by herself away from home. This idea that she's on a visit won't wash any longer. Now finish that letter —"worthy, but you may rest assured that I shall do my best to sustain the—er—dignity of the office."

[MAUD *types desperately.*

Got that? "And—er—preserve the tradition so worthily——" No—"so staunchly"—er—er——

MAUD. Upheld.

BUILDER. Ah! "—upheld by yourself.—Faithfully yours."

MAUD. [*Finishing*] Father, you thought Athene went off in a huff. It wasn't that a bit. She always meant to go. She just got you into a rage to make it easier. She *hated* living at *home.*

BUILDER. Nonsense! Why on earth should she?

MAUD. Well, she did! And so do—— [*Checking herself*] And so you see it'll only make you ridiculous to go.

BUILDER. [*Rises*] Now what's behind this, Maud?

MAUD. Behind—— Oh! nothing!

BUILDER. The fact is, you girls have been spoiled, and you enjoy twisting my tail; but you can't make me roar this morning. I'm too pleased with things. You'll see, it'll be all right with Athene.

MAUD. [*Very suddenly*] Father!

BUILDER. [*Grimly humorous*] Well! Get it off your chest. What's that letter about?

MAUD. [*Failing again and crumpling the letter behind her back*] Oh! nothing.

BUILDER. Everything's nothing this morning. Do you know what sort of people Athene associates with now—I suppose you see her?

MAUD. Sometimes.

BUILDER. Well?

MAUD. Nobody much. There isn't anybody here to associate with. It's all hopelessly behind the times.

BUILDER. Oh! you think so! That's the inflammatory fiction you pick up. I tell you what, young woman—the sooner you and your sister get rid of your silly notions about not living at home, and making your own way, the sooner you'll both get married and make it. Men don't like the new spirit in women—they may say they do, but they don't.

MAUD. *You* don't, father, I know.

BUILDER. Well, I'm very ordinary. If you keep your eyes open, you'll soon see that.

MAUD. Men don't like freedom for anybody but themselves.

BUILDER. That's not the way to put it. [*Tapping out his pipe*] Women in your class have never had to face realities.

MAUD. No, but we want to.

BUILDER. [*Good-humouredly*] Well, I'll bet you what you like, Athene's dose of reality will have cured her.

MAUD. And I'll bet you—— No, I won't!

BUILDER. You'd better not. Athene will come home, and only too glad to do it. Ring for Topping and order the car at twelve.

As he opens the door to pass out, MAUD *starts forward, but checks herself.*

MAUD. [*Looking at her watch*] Half-past eleven! Good heavens!

She goes to the bell and rings. Then goes back to the table, and writes an address on a bit of paper.

[TOPPING *enters Right.*

TOPPING. Did you ring, Miss?

MAUD. [*With the paper*] Yes. Look here, Topping! Can you manage—on your bicycle—now at once? I want to send a message to Miss Athene—awfully important. It's just this: "Look out! Father is coming." [*Holding out the paper*] Here's her address. You must get there and away again by twelve. Father and mother want the car then to go there. Order it before you go. It won't take you twenty minutes on your bicycle. It's down by the river near the ferry. But you mustn't be seen by them either going or coming.

TOPPING. If I should fall into their hands, Miss, shall I eat the despatch?

MAUD. Rather! You're a brick, Topping. Hurry up!

TOPPING. Nothing more precise, Miss?

MAUD. M—m—— No.

TOPPING. Very good, Miss Maud. [*Conning the address*] "Briary Studio, River Road. Look out! Father is coming!" I'll go out the back way. Any answer?

MAUD. No.

[TOPPING *nods his head and goes out.*

MAUD. [*To herself*] Well, it's all I can do.

[*She stands, considering, as the* CURTAIN *falls.*

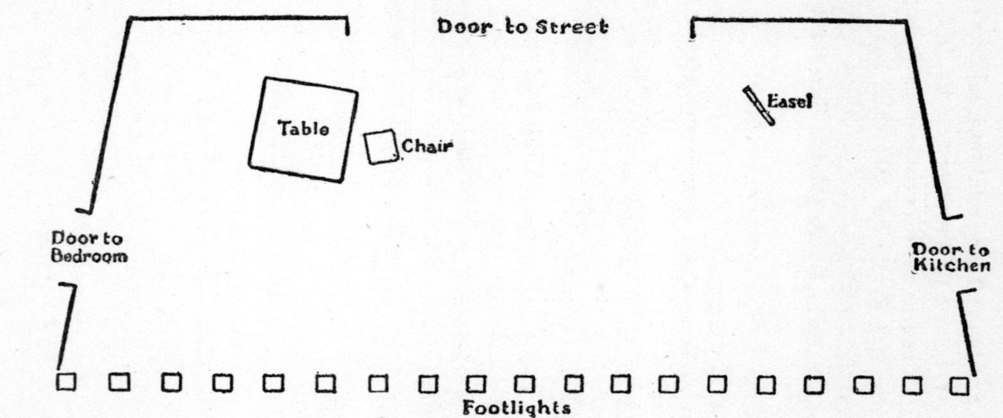
Door to Street
Table
Chair
Easel
Door to Bedroom
Door to Kitchen
Footlights

SCENE II

The Studio, to which are attached living rooms, might be rented at eighty pounds a year—some painting and gear indeed, but an air of life rather than of work. Things strewn about. Bare walls, a sloping skylight, no windows; no fireplace visible; a bedroom door, stage Right; a kitchen door, stage Left. A door, Centre back, into the street. The door knocker is going.

From the kitchen door, Left, comes the very young person, ANNIE, *in blotting-paper blue linen, with a white Dutch cap. She is pretty, her cheeks rosy, and her forehead puckered. She opens the street door. Standing outside is* TOPPING. *He steps in a pace or two.*

TOPPING. Miss Builder live here?

ANNIE. Oh! no, sir; Mrs. Herringhame.

TOPPING. Mrs. Herringhame? Oh! young lady with dark hair and large expressive eyes?

ANNIE. Oh! yes, sir.

TOPPING. With an "A. B." on her linen?

[*Moves to table.*

ANNIE. Yes, sir.

TOPPING. And "Athene Builder" on her drawings?

ANNIE. [*Looking at one*] Yes, sir.

TOPPING. Let's see. [*He examines the drawing*] Mrs. Herringhame, you said?

ANNIE. Oh! yes, sir.

TOPPING. Wot oh!

ANNIE. Did you want anything, sir?

TOPPING. Drop the "sir," my dear; I'm the Builders' man. Mr. Herringhame in?

ANNIE. Oh! no, sir.

TOPPING. Take a message. I can't wait. From Miss Maud Builder. "Look out! Father is coming." Now, whichever of 'em comes in first—that's the message, and don't you forget it.

ANNIE. Oh! no, sir.

TOPPING. So they're married?

ANNIE. Oh! I don't know, sir.

TOPPING. I see. Well, it ain't known to Builder, J.P., either. That's why there's a message. See?

ANNIE. Oh! yes, sir.

TOPPING. Keep your head. I must hop it. From Miss Maud Builder. "Look out! Father is coming."

He nods, turns and goes, pulling the door to behind him. ANNIE *stands "baff" for a moment.*

ANNIE. Ah!

She goes across to the bedroom on the Right, and soon returns with a suit of pyjamas, a toothbrush, a pair of slippers and a case of razors, which she puts on the table, and disappears into the kitchen. She reappears with a bread pan, which she deposits in the centre of the room; then crosses again to the bedroom, and once more reappears with a clothes brush, two hair brushes, and a Norfolk jacket. As she stuffs all these into the bread pan and bears it back into the kitchen, there is the sound of a car driving up and stopping. ANNIE *reappears at the kitchen door just as the knocker sounds.*

ANNIE. Vexin' and provokin'! [*Knocker again. She opens the door*] Oh!

[MR. *and* MRS. BUILDER *enter.*

BUILDER. Mr. and Mrs. Builder. My daughter in?

ANNIE. [*Confounded*] Oh! sir, no, sir.

BUILDER. My good girl, not "Oh! sir, no, sir." Simply: No, sir. See?

ANNIE. Oh! sir, yes, sir.

BUILDER. Where is she?

ANNIE. Oh! sir, I don't know, sir.

BUILDER. [*Fixing her as though he suspected her of banter*] Will she be back soon?

ANNIE. No, sir.

BUILDER. How do you know?

ANNIE. I d-don't, sir.

BUILDER. Then why do you say so? [*About to mutter "She's an idiot!" he looks at her blushing face and panting figure, pats her on the shoulder and says*] Never mind; don't be nervous.

ANNIE. Oh! yes, sir. Is that all, please, sir?

MRS. BUILDER. [*With a side look at her husband and a faint smile*] Yes; you can go.

ANNIE. Thank you, ma'am.

She turns and hurries out into the kitchen, Left. BUILDER *gazes after her, and* MRS. BUILDER *gazes at* BUILDER *with her faint smile.*

BUILDER. [*After the girl is gone*] Quaint and Dutch—pretty little figure! [*Staring round*] H'm! Extraordinary girls are! Fancy Athene preferring this to home. What?

MRS. BUILDER. I didn't say anything.

BUILDER. [*Placing a chair for his wife, and sitting down himself*] Well, we must wait, I suppose. Confound that Nixon legacy! If Athene hadn't had that potty little legacy left her, she couldn't have done this. Well, I daresay it's all spent by now. I made a mistake to lose my temper with her.

MRS. BUILDER. Isn't it always a mistake to lose one's temper?

BUILDER. That's very nice and placid; sort of thing you women who live sheltered lives can say. I often wonder if you women realise the strain on a business man.

MRS. BUILDER. [*In her softly ironical voice*] It seems a shame to add the strain of family life.

BUILDER. You've always been so passive. When I want a thing, I've got to have it.

MRS. BUILDER. I've noticed that.

BUILDER. [*With a short laugh*] Odd if you hadn't

in twenty-three years. [*Touching a canvas standing against the chair with his toe*] Art! Just a pretext. We shall be having Maud wanting to cut loose next. She's very restive. Still, I oughtn't to have had that scene with Athene. I ought to have put quiet pressure.

[MRS. BUILDER *smiles.*

BUILDER. What are you smiling at?

[MRS. BUILDER *shrugs her shoulders.*

Look at this—— Cigarettes! [*He examines the brand on the box*] Strong, very—and not good! [*He opens the door*] Kitchen! [*He shuts it, crosses, and opens the door, Right*] Bedroom!

MRS. BUILDER. [*To his disappearing form*] Do you think you ought, John?

He has disappeared, and she ends with an expressive movement of her hands, a long sigh, and a closing of her eyes. BUILDER'S *peremptory voice is heard: "Julia!"*

What now? [*She follows into the bedroom.*

The maid ANNIE *puts her head out of the kitchen door; she comes out a step as if to fly; then, at* BUILDER'S *voice, shrinks back into the kitchen.*

BUILDER, *reappearing with a razor strop in one hand and a shaving-brush in the other, is followed by* MRS. BUILDER.

BUILDER. Explain these! My God! Where's that girl?

MRS. BUILDER. John! Don't! [*Getting between him and the kitchen door*] It's not dignified.

BUILDER. I don't care a damn.

MRS. BUILDER. John, you mustn't. Athene has the tiny beginning of a moustache, you know.

BUILDER. What! I shall stay and clear this up if I have to wait a week. Men who let their daughters ——! This age is the limit.

He makes a vicious movement with the strop, as though laying it across someone's back.

MRS. BUILDER. She would never stand that. Even wives object, nowadays.

BUILDER. [*Grimly*] The war's upset everything. Women are utterly out of hand. Why the deuce doesn't she come?

MRS. BUILDER. Suppose you leave me here to see her.

BUILDER. [*Ominously*] This is my job.

MRS. BUILDER. I think it's more mine.

BUILDER. Don't stand there opposing everything I say! I'll go and have another look—— [*He is going towards the bedroom when the sound of a latchkey in the outer door arrests him. He puts the strop and brush behind his back, and adds in a low voice*] Here she is!

MRS. BUILDER *has approached him, and they have both turned towards the opening door.* GUY HERRINGHAME *comes in. They are a little out of his line of sight, and he has shut the door before he sees them. When he does, his mouth falls open, and his hand on to the knob of the door. He is a comely young man in Harris tweeds. Moreover, he is smoking. He would speak if he could, but his surprise is too excessive.*

BUILDER. Well, sir?

GUY. [*Recovering a little*] I was about to say the same to you, sir.

BUILDER. [*Very red from repression*] These rooms are not yours, are they?

GUY. Nor yours, sir?

BUILDER. May I ask if you know whose they are?

GUY. My sister's.

BUILDER. Your—you——!

MRS. BUILDER. John!

BUILDER. Will you kindly tell me why your sister signs her drawings by the name of my daughter, Athene Builder—and has a photograph of my wife hanging there?

The YOUNG MAN *looks at* MRS. BUILDER *and winces, but recovers himself.*

GUY. [*Boldly*] As a matter of fact this *is* my sister's studio; she's in France—and has a friend staying here.

BUILDER. Oh! And you have a key?

GUY. My sister's.

BUILDER. Does your sister shave?

GUY. I—I don't think so.

BUILDER. No. Then perhaps you'll tell me what these mean?

[*He takes out the strop and shaving stick.*

GUY. Oh! Ah! Those things?

BUILDER. Yes. Now then?

GUY. [*Addressing* MRS. BUILDER] Need we go into this in your presence, ma'am? It seems rather delicate.

BUILDER. What explanation have you got?

GUY. Well, you see——

BUILDER. No lies; out with it!

GUY. [*With decision*] I prefer to say nothing.

BUILDER. What's your name?

GUY. Guy Herringhame.

BUILDER. Do you live here?

[GUY *makes no sign.*

MRS. BUILDER. [*To* GUY] I think you had better go.

BUILDER. Julia, *will* you leave me to manage this?

MRS. BUILDER. [*To* GUY] When do you expect my daughter in?

GUY. Now—directly.

MRS. BUILDER. [*Quietly*] Are you married to her?

GUY. Yes. That is—no-o; not altogether, I mean.

BUILDER. What's that? Say that again!

GUY. [*Folding his arms*] I'm not going to say another word.

BUILDER. I am.

MRS. BUILDER. John—please!

BUILDER. Don't put your oar in! I've had wonderful patience so far. [*He puts his foot through a drawing*] Art! This is what comes of it! Are *you* an artist?

GUY. No; a flying man. The truth is——

BUILDER. I don't want to hear *you* speak the truth. I'll wait for my daughter.

GUY. If you do, I hope you'll be so very good as to be gentle. If you get angry I might too, and that would be awfully ugly.

BUILDER. Well, I'm damned!

GUY. I quite understand that, sir. But, as a man of the world, I hope you'll take a pull before she comes, if you mean to stay.

BUILDER. *If* we mean to stay! That's good!

GUY. Will you have a cigarette?

BUILDER. I—I can't express——

GUY. [*Soothingly*] Don't try, sir. [*He jerks up his chin, listening*] I think that's her. [*Goes to the door*] Yes. Now, please! [*He opens the door*] Your father and mother, Athene.

ATHENE *enters. She is flushed and graceful. Twenty-two, with a short upper lip, a straight nose, dark hair, and glowing eyes. She wears bright colours, and has a slow, musical voice, with a slight lisp.*

ATHENE. Oh! How are you, mother dear? This is rather a surprise. Father always keeps his word, so I certainly didn't expect *him*.

She looks steadfastly at BUILDER, *but does not approach.*

BUILDER. [*Controlling himself with an effort*] Now, Athene, what's this?

ATHENE. What's what?

BUILDER. [*The strop held out*] Are you married to this—this——?

ATHENE. [*Quietly*] To all intents and purposes.

BUILDER. In law?

ATHENE. No.

BUILDER. My God! You—you——!

ATHENE. Father, don't call names, please.

BUILDER. Why aren't you married to him?

ATHENE. Do you want a lot of reasons, or the real one?

BUILDER. This is maddening! [*Goes up stage.*

ATHENE. Mother dear, will you go into the other room with Guy? [*She points to the door Right.*

BUILDER. Why?

ATHENE. Because I would rather she didn't hear the reason.

GUY. [*To* ATHENE, *sotto voce*] He's not safe.

ATHENE. Oh! yes; go on.

GUY *follows* MRS. BUILDER, *and after hesitation at the door they go out into the bedroom.*

BUILDER. Now then!

ATHENE. Well, father, if you want to know the real reason, it's—you.

BUILDER. What on earth do you mean?

ATHENE. Guy wants to marry me. In fact, we—— But I had such a scunner of marriage from watching you at home, that I——

BUILDER. Don't be impudent! My patience is at breaking-point, I warn you.

ATHENE. I'm perfectly serious, Father. I tell you, we meant to marry, but so far I haven't been able to bring myself to it. You never noticed how we children have watched you.

BUILDER. Me?

ATHENE. Yes. You and mother, and other things; all sorts of things——

BUILDER. [*Taking out a handkerchief and wiping his brow*] I really think you're mad.

ATHENE. I'm sure you must, dear.

BUILDER. Don't "dear" me! What have you noticed? D'you mean I'm not a good husband and father?

ATHENE. Look at mother. I suppose you can't, now; you're too used to her.

BUILDER. Of course I'm used to her. What else is marrying for?

ATHENE. That; and the production of such as me. And it isn't good enough, father. You shouldn't have set us such a perfect example.

BUILDER. You're talking the most arrant nonsense I ever heard. [*He lifts his hands*] I've a good mind to shake it out of you.

ATHENE. Shall I call Guy? [*He drops his hands.* Confess that being a good husband and father has tried you terribly. It has *us*, you know.

BUILDER. [*Taking refuge in sarcasm*] When you've quite done being funny, perhaps you'll tell me why you've behaved like a common street flapper.

ATHENE. [*Simply*] I couldn't bear to think of Guy as a family man. That's all—absolutely. It's not *his* fault; he's been awfully anxious to be one.

BUILDER. You've disgraced us, then; that's what it comes to.

ATHENE. I don't want to be unkind, but you've brought it on yourself.

BUILDER. [*Genuinely distracted*] I can't even get a glimmer of what you mean. I've never been anything but firm. Impatient, perhaps. I'm not an angel; no ordinary healthy man is. I've never grudged you girls any comfort, or pleasure.

ATHENE. Except wills of our own.

BUILDER. What do you want with wills of your own till you're married?

ATHENE. You forget mother!

BUILDER. What about her?

ATHENE. She's very married. Has she a will of her own?

BUILDER. [*Sullenly*] She's learnt to know when I'm in the right.

ATHENE. I don't ever mean to learn to know when Guy's in the right. Mother's forty-one, and twenty-three years of that she's been your wife. It's a long time, father. Don't you ever look at her face?

BUILDER. [*Troubled in a remote way*] Rubbish!

ATHENE. I didn't want my face to get like that.

BUILDER. With such views about marriage, what business had you to go near a man? Come, now!

ATHENE. Because I fell in love.

BUILDER. Love leads to marriage—and to nothing else, but the streets. What an example to your sister!

ATHENE. You don't know Maud any more than you knew me. She's got a will of her own too, I can tell you.

BUILDER. Now, look here, Athene. It's always been my way to face accomplished facts. What's done can't be undone; but it can be remedied. You must marry this young —— at once, before it gets out. He's behaved like a ruffian: but, by your own confession, you've behaved worse. You've been bitten by this modern disease, this—this utter lack of common decency. There's an eternal order in certain things, and marriage is one of them; in fact, it's the chief. Come, now. Give me a promise, and I'll try my utmost to forget the whole thing.

ATHENE. When we quarrelled, father, you said you didn't care what became of me.

BUILDER. I was angry.

ATHENE. So you are now.

BUILDER. Come, Athene, don't be childish! Promise me!

ATHENE. [*With a little shudder*] No! We were on the edge of it. But now I've seen you again—— Poor mother!

BUILDER. [*Very angry*] This is simply blasphemous. What do you mean by harping on your mother? If you think that—that—she doesn't—that she isn't——

ATHENE. Now, father!

BUILDER. I'm damned if I'll sit down under this injustice. Your mother is—is pretty irritating, I can tell you. She—she—— Everything suppressed. And—and no—blood in her!

ATHENE. I knew it!

BUILDER. [*Aware that he has confirmed some thought*

in her that he had no intention of confirming] What's that?

Athene. Don't you ever look at your own face, father? When you shave, for instance.

Builder. Of course I do.

Athene. It isn't satisfied, is it?

Builder. I don't know what on earth you mean.

Athene. You can't help it, but you'd be ever so much happier if you were a Mohammedan, and two or three, instead of one, had—had learned to know when you were in the right.

Builder. 'Pon my soul! This is outrageous!

Athene. Truth often is.

Builder. Will you be quiet?

Athene. I don't ever want to feel sorry for Guy in that way.

Builder. I think you're the most immodest—— I'm ashamed that you're my daughter. If your mother had ever carried on as you are now——

Athene. Would you have been firm with her?

Builder. [*Really sick at heart at this unwonted mockery which meets him at every turn*] Be quiet, you——!

Athene. Has mother never turned?

Builder. You're an unnatural girl! Go your own way to hell!

Athene. I am not coming back *home*, father.

Builder. [*Wrenching open the door, Right*] Julia! Come! We can't stay here.

[Mrs. Builder *comes forth, followed by* Guy.

As for you, sir, if you start by allowing a woman to impose her crazy ideas about marriage on you, all I can say is—I despise you. [*He crosses to the outer door, followed by his wife. To* ATHENE] I've done with *you!* [*He goes out.*

MRS. BUILDER, *who has so far seemed to accompany him, shuts the door quickly and remains in the studio. She stands there with that faint smile on her face, looking at the two young people.*

ATHENE. Awfully sorry, mother; but don't you see what a scunner father's given me?

MRS. BUILDER. My dear, all men are not alike.

GUY. I've always told her that, ma'am.

ATHENE. [*Softly*] Oh! mother, I'm so sorry for you.

The handle of the door is rattled, a fist is beaten on it.

[*She stamps, and covers her ears*] Disgusting!

GUY. Shall I——?

MRS. BUILDER. [*Shaking her head*] I'm going in a moment. [*To* ATHENE] You owe it to me, Athene.

ATHENE. Oh! if somebody would give him a lesson! [BUILDER'S *voice: "Julia!"*

Have you ever tried, mother?

MRS. BUILDER *looks at the* YOUNG MAN, *who turns away out of hearing.*

MRS. BUILDER. Athene, you're mistaken. I've always stood up to him in my own way.

ATHENE. Oh! but, mother—listen!

The beating and rattling have recommenced, and the voice: "Are you coming?"

[*Passionately*] And that's family life! Father was all right before he married, I expect. And now it's like this. How you survive——!

MRS. BUILDER. He's only in a passion, my dear.

ATHENE. It's wicked.

MRS. BUILDER. It doesn't work otherwise, Athene.

[*A single loud bang on the door.*

ATHENE. If he beats on that door again, I shall scream.

MRS. BUILDER *smiles, shakes her head, and turns to the door.*

MRS. BUILDER. Now, my dear, you're going to be sensible, to please me. It's really best. If *I* say so, it must be. It's all comedy, Athene.

ATHENE. Tragedy!

GUY. [*Turning to them*] Look here! Shall I shift him?

MRS. BUILDER *shakes her head and opens the door.* BUILDER *stands there, a furious figure.*

BUILDER. Will you come, and leave that baggage and her cad?

MRS. BUILDER *steps quickly out and the door is closed.* GUY *makes an angry movement towards it.*

ATHENE. Guy!

GUY. [*Turning to her*] That puts the top hat on. So persuasive! [*He takes out of his pocket a wedding ring, and a marriage licence*] Well! What's to be done with these pretty things, now?

ATHENE. Burn them!

GUY. [*Slowly*] Not quite. You can't imagine I should ever be like that, Athene?

ATHENE. Marriage does wonders.

GUY. Thanks.

ATHENE. Oh! Guy, don't be horrid. I feel awfully bad.

GUY. Well, what do you think I feel? "Cad!"

They turn to see ANNIE *in hat and coat, with a suit-case in her hand, coming from the door Left.*

ANNIE. Oh! ma'am, please, Miss, I want to go home.

GUY. [*Exasperated*] She wants to go home—she wants to go home!

ATHENE. Guy! All right, Annie.

ANNIE. Oh! thank you, Miss.

[*She moves across in front of them.*

ATHENE. [*Suddenly*] Annie!

[ANNIE *stops and turns to her.*

What are you afraid of?

ANNIE. [*With comparative boldness*] I—I might catch it, Miss.

ATHENE. From your people?

ANNIE. Oh! no, Miss; from you. You see, I've got a young man that wants to marry me. And if I don't let him, I might get into trouble meself.

ATHENE. What sort of father and mother have you got, Annie?

ANNIE. I never thought, Miss. And of course I don't want to begin.

ATHENE. D'you mean you've never noticed how they treat each other?

ANNIE. I don't think they do, Miss.

ATHENE. Exactly.

ANNIE. They haven't time. Father's an engine driver.

GUY. And what's your young man, Annie?

ANNIE. [*Embarrassed*] Somethin' like you, sir. But very respectable.

ATHENE. And suppose you marry him, and he treats you like a piece of furniture?

ANNIE. I—I could treat him the same, Miss.

ATHENE. Don't you believe that, Annie!

ANNIE. He's very mild.

ATHENE. That's because he wants you. You wait till he doesn't.

[ANNIE *looks at* GUY.

GUY. Don't you believe her, Annie; if he's decent——

ANNIE. Oh! yes, sir.

ATHENE. [*Suppressing a smile*] Of course—but the point is, Annie, that marriage makes all the difference.

ANNIE. Yes, Miss; that's what I thought.

ATHENE. You don't see. What I mean is that when once he's sure of you, he may change completely.

ANNIE. [*Slowly, looking at her thumb*] Oh! I don't—think—he'll hammer me, Miss. Of course, I know you can't tell till you've found out.

ATHENE. Well, I've no right to influence you.

ANNIE. Oh! no, Miss; that's what I've been thinking.

GUY. You're quite right, Annie—this is no place for you.

ANNIE. You see, we can't be married, sir, till he gets his rise. So it'll be a continual temptation to me.

ATHENE. Well, all right, Annie. I hope you'll never regret it.

ANNIE. Oh! no, Miss.

GUY. I say, Annie, don't go away thinking evil of us; we didn't realise you knew we weren't married.

ATHENE. We certainly did not.

ANNIE. Oh! I didn't think it right to take notice.

GUY. We beg your pardon.

ANNIE. Oh! no, sir. Only, seein' Mr. and Mrs. Builder so upset, brought it 'ome like. And father *can* be 'andy with a strap.

ATHENE. There you are! *Force majeure!*

ANNIE. Oh! yes, Miss.

ATHENE. Well, good-bye, Annie. What are you going to say to your people?

ANNIE. Oh! I shan't say I've been livin' in a family that wasn't a family, Miss. It wouldn't do no good.

ATHENE. Well, here are your wages.

ANNIE. Oh! I'm puttin' you out, Miss.

[*She takes the money.*

ATHENE. Nonsense, Annie. And here's your fare home.

ANNIE. Oh! thank you, Miss. I'm very sorry. Of course if you was to change your mind——

[*She stops, embarrassed.*

ATHENE. I don't think——

GUY. [*Abruptly*] Good-bye, Annie. Here's five bob for the movies.

ANNIE. Oh! good-bye, sir, and thank you. I was goin' there now with my young man. He's just round the corner.

GUY. Be very careful of him.

ANNIE. Oh! yes, sir, I will. Good-bye, sir. Good-bye, Miss. [*She goes.*

GUY. So *her* father has a firm hand too. But it takes *her* back to the nest. How's that, Athene?

ATHENE. [*Playing with a leathern button on his coat*] If you'd watched it ever since you could watch anything, seen it kill out all—— It's having power that does it. I know Father's got awfully good points.

GUY. Well, they don't stick out.

ATHENE. He works fearfully hard; he's upright, and plucky. He's not stingy. But he's smothered his animal nature—and that's done it. I don't want to see you smother anything, Guy.

GUY. [*Gloomily*] I suppose one never knows what one's got under the lid. If he hadn't come here to-day—— [*He spins the wedding ring*] He certainly gives one pause. Used he to whack you?

ATHENE. Yes.

GUY. Brute!

ATHENE. With the best intentions. You see, he's a Town Councillor, and a magistrate. I suppose they *have* to be "*firm.*" Maud and I sneaked in once to listen to him. There was a woman who came for protection from her husband. If he'd known we were there, he'd have had a fit.

GUY. Did he give her the protection?

ATHENE. Yes; he gave her back to the husband. Wasn't it—English?

GUY. [*With a grunt*] Hang it! We're not all like that.

ATHENE. [*Twisting his button*] I think it's really a sense of property so deep that they don't know they've got it. Father can *talk* about freedom like a—politician.

GUY. [*Fitting the wedding ring on her finger*] Well! Let's see how it looks, anyway.

ATHENE. Don't play with fire, Guy.

GUY. There's something in atavism, darling; there really is. I like it—I do. [*A knock at the door.*

ATHENE. That sounds like Annie again. Just see.

GUY. [*Opening the door*] It is. Come in, Annie. What's wrong now?

ANNIE. [*Entering in confusion*] Oh! sir, please, sir—I've told my young man.

ATHENE. Well, what does he say?

ANNIE. 'E was 'orrified, Miss.

GUY. The deuce he was! At our conduct?

ANNIE. Oh! no, sir—at mine.

ATHENE. But you did your best; you left us.

ANNIE. Oh! yes, Miss; that's why 'e's horrified.

GUY. Good for your young man.

ANNIE. [*Flattered*] Yes, sir. 'E said I 'ad no strength of mind.

ATHENE. So you want to come back?

ANNIE. Oh! yes, Miss.

ATHENE. All right.

GUY. But what about catching it?

ANNIE. Oh, sir, 'e said there was nothing like Epsom salts.

GUY. He's a wag, your young man.

ANNIE. He was in the Army, sir.

GUY. You said he was respectable.

ANNIE. Oh! yes, sir; but not so respectable as that.

ATHENE. Well, Annie, get your things off, and lay lunch.

ANNIE. Oh! yes, Miss.

She makes a little curtsey and passes through into the kitchen.

GUY. Strength of mind! Have a little, Athene—won't you?

[*He holds out the marriage licence before her.*

ATHENE. I don't know—I don't know! If—it turned out——

GUY. It won't. Come on. Must take chances in this life.

ATHENE. [*Looking up into his face*] Guy, promise me—solemnly that you'll never let me stand in your way, or stand in mine!

GUY. Right! That's a bargain.

[*They embrace.*

ATHENE *quivers towards him. They embrace fervently as* ANNIE *enters with the bread pan. They spring apart.*

ANNIE. Oh!

GUY. It's all right, Annie. There's only one more day's infection before you. We're to be married to-morrow morning.

ANNIE. Oh! yes, sir. Won't Mr. Builder be pleased?

GUY. H'm! That's not exactly our reason.

ANNIE. [*Right*] Oh! no, sir. Of course you can't be a family without, can you?

GUY. What have you got in that thing?

ANNIE *is moving across with the bread pan. She halts at the bedroom door.*

ANNIE. Oh! please, ma'am, I was to give you a message—very important—from Miss Maud Builder: "Look out! Father is coming!" [*She goes out.*

The CURTAIN *falls.*

ACT II

ACT II

BUILDER'S *study. At the table,* MAUD *has just put a sheet of paper into a typewriter. She sits facing the audience, with her hands stretched over the keys.*

MAUD. [*To herself*] I must get that expression.

Her face assumes a furtive, listening look. Then she gets up, whisks to the mirror over the fireplace, scrutinises the expression in it, and going back to the table, sits down again with hands outstretched above the keys, and an accentuation of the expression. The door up Left is opened, and TOPPING *appears. He looks at* MAUD, *who just turns her eyes.*

TOPPING. Lunch has been ready some time, Miss Maud.

MAUD. I don't want any lunch. Did you give it?

TOPPING. Miss Athene was out. I gave the message to a young party. She looked a bit green, Miss. I hope nothing'll go wrong with the works. Shall I keep lunch back?

MAUD. If something's gone wrong, they won't have any appetite, Topping.

TOPPING. If you think I might risk it, Miss, I'd like to slip round to my dentist.

[*He lays a finger on his cheek.*

MAUD. [*Smiling*] Oh! What race is being run this afternoon, then, Topping?

TOPPING. [*Twinkling, and shifting his finger to the side of his nose*] Well, I don't suppose you've 'eard of it, Miss; but as a matter of fact it's the Cesarwitch.

MAUD. Got anything on?

TOPPING. Only my shirt, Miss.

MAUD. Is it a good thing, then?

TOPPING. I've seen worse roll up. [*With a touch of enthusiasm*] Dark horse, Miss Maud, at twenty to one.

MAUD. Put me ten bob on, Topping. I want all the money I can get, just now.

TOPPING. You're not the first, Miss.

MAUD. I say, Topping, do you know anything about the film?

TOPPING. [*Nodding*] Rather a specialty of mine, Miss.

MAUD. Well, just stand there, and give me your opinion of this.

[TOPPING *moves down Left.*

She crouches over the typewriter, lets her hands play on the keys; stops; assumes that listening, furtive look; listens again, and lets her head go slowly round, preceded by her eyes; breaks it off, and says:

What should you say I was?

TOPPING. Guilty, Miss.

MAUD. [*With triumph*] There! Then you think I've got it?

TOPPING. Well, of course, I couldn't say just what sort of a crime you'd committed, but I should think pretty 'ot stuff.

MAUD. Yes; I've got them here.

[*She pats her chest.*

TOPPING. Really, Miss.

MAUD. Yes. There's just one point, Topping; it's psychological.

TOPPING. Indeed, Miss?

MAUD. Should I naturally put my hand on them; or would there be a reaction quick enough to stop me? You see, I'm alone—and the point is whether the fear of being seen would stop me although I knew I couldn't be seen. It's rather subtle.

TOPPING. I think there's be a rehaction, Miss.

MAUD. So do I. To touch them [*She clasps her chest*] is a bit obvious, isn't it?

TOPPING. If the haudience knows you've got 'em there.

MAUD. Oh! yes, it's seen me put them. Look here, I'll show you that too.

She opens an imaginary drawer, takes out some bits of sealing-wax, and with every circumstance of stealth in face and hands, conceals them in her bosom.

All right?

TOPPING. [*Nodding*] Fine, Miss. You *have* got a film face. What *are* they, if I may ask?

MAUD. [*Reproducing the sealing-wax*] The Fanshawe diamonds. There's just one thing here too, Topping.

In real life, which should I naturally do—put them in here [*She touches her chest*] or in my bag?

TOPPING. [*Touching his waistcoat—earnestly*] Well! To put 'em in *here*, Miss, I should say is more—more pishchological.

MAUD. [*Subduing her lips*] Yes; but——

TOPPING. You see, then you've got 'em on you.

MAUD. But that's just the point. Shouldn't I naturally think: Safer in my bag; then I can pretend somebody put them there. You see, nobody could put them on me.

TOPPING. Well, I should say that depends on your character. Of course I don't know what your character is.

MAUD. No; that's the beastly part of it—the author doesn't, either. It's all left to me.

TOPPING. In that case, I should please myself, Miss. To put 'em in 'ere's warmer.

MAUD. Yes, I think you're right. It's more human.

TOPPING. I didn't know you 'ad a taste this way, Miss Maud.

MAUD. More than a taste, Topping—a talent.

TOPPING. Well, in my belief, we all have a vice about us somewhere. But if I were you, Miss, I wouldn't touch bettin', not with this other on you. You might get to feel a bit crowded.

MAUD. Well, then, only put the ten bob on if you're *sure* he's going to win. You can post the money on after me. I'll send you an address, Topping, because I shan't be here.

TOPPING. [*Disturbed*] What! You're not going, too, Miss Maud?

MAUD. To seek my fortune.

TOPPING. Oh! Hang it all, Miss, think of what you'll leave behind. Miss Athene's leavin' home has made it pretty steep, but this'll touch bottom—this will.

MAUD. Yes; I expect you'll find it rather difficult for a bit when I'm gone. Miss Baldini, you know. I've been studying with her. She's got me this chance with the movie people. I'm going on trial as the guilty typist in "The Heartache of Miranda."

TOPPING. [*Surprised out of politeness*] Well, I never! That does sound like 'em! Are you goin' to tell the guv'nor, Miss?

[MAUD *nods.*

In that case, I think I'll be gettin' off to my dentist before the band plays.

MAUD. All right, Topping; hope you won't lose a tooth.

TOPPING. [*With a grin*] It's on the knees of the gods, Miss, as they say in the headlines.

[*He goes.* MAUD *stretches herself and listens.*

MAUD. I believe that's them. Shivery funky.

[*She runs off up Left.*

BUILDER. [*Entering from the hall and crossing to the fireplace*] Monstrous! Really monstrous!

CAMILLE *enters from the hall. She has a little collecting book in her hand.*

BUILDER. Well, Camille?

CAMILLE. A sistare from the Sacred 'Eart, Monsieur —her little book for the orphan children.

BUILDER. I can't be bothered—*What is it?*

CAMILLE. Orphan, Monsieur.

BUILDER. H'm! Well! [*Feeling in his breast pocket*] Give her that. [*He hands her a five-pound note.*

CAMILLE. I am sure she will be veree grateful for the poor little beggars. Madame says she will not be coming to lunch, Monsieur.

BUILDER. *I* don't want any, either. Tell Topping I'll have some coffee.

CAMILLE. Topping has gone to the dentist, Monsieur; 'e 'as the toothache.

BUILDER. Toothache—poor devil! H'm! I'm expecting my brother, but I don't know that I can see him.

CAMILLE. No, Monsieur?

BUILDER. Ask your mistress to come here.

He looks up, and catching her eye, looks away.

CAMILLE. Yes, Monsieur.

As she turns he looks swiftly at her, sweeping her up and down. She turns her head and catches his glance, which is swiftly dropped.

Will Monsieur not 'ave anything to eat?

BUILDER. [*Shaking his head—abruptly*] No. Bring the coffee!

CAMILLE. Is Monsieur not well?

BUILDER. Yes—quite well.

CAMILLE. [*Sweetening her eyes*] A cutlet soubise? No?

BUILDER. [*With a faint response in his eyes, instantly subdued*] Nothing! nothing!

CAMILLE. And Madame nothing too—Tt! Tt!

With her hand on the door she looks back, again catches his eyes in an engagement instantly broken off, and goes out.

BUILDER. [*Stock-still, and staring at the door*] That girl's a continual irritation to me! She's dangerous! What a life! I believe that girl——

The door Left is opened and MRS. BUILDER *comes in.*

BUILDER. There's some coffee coming; do your head good. Look here, Julia. I'm sorry I beat on that door. I apologize. I was in a towering passion. I wish I didn't get into these rages. But—dash it all——! I couldn't walk away and leave you there.

MRS. BUILDER. Why not?

BUILDER. You keep everything to yourself, so; I never have any notion what you're thinking. What *did* you say to her?

MRS. BUILDER. Told her it would never work.

BUILDER. Well, that's something. She's crazy. D'you suppose she was telling the truth about that young blackguard wanting to marry her?

MRS. BUILDER. I'm sure of it.

BUILDER. When you think of how she's been brought up. You would have thought that religion alone——

MRS. BUILDER. The girls haven't *wanted* to go to church for years. They've always said they didn't see why they should go to keep up your position. I don't know if you remember that you once caned them for running off on a Sunday morning.

BUILDER. Well?

MRS. BUILDER. They've never had any religion since.

BUILDER. H'm! [*He takes a short turn up the room*] What's to be done about Athene?

MRS. BUILDER. You said you had done *with* her.

BUILDER. You know I didn't mean that. I might just as well have said I'd done with you! Apply your wits, Julia! At any moment this thing may come out. In a little town like this you can keep nothing dark. How can I take this nomination for Mayor?

MRS. BUILDER. Perhaps Ralph could help.

BUILDER. What? His daughters have never done anything disgraceful, and his wife's a pattern.

MRS. BUILDER. Yes; Ralph isn't at all a family man.

BUILDER. [*Staring at her*] I do wish you wouldn't turn things upside down in that ironical way. It isn't—English.

MRS. BUILDER. I can't help having been born in Jersey.

BUILDER. No; I suppose it's in your blood. The French—— [*He stops short.*

MRS. BUILDER. Yes?

BUILDER. Very irritating sometimes to a plain Englishman—that's all.

MRS. BUILDER. Shall I get rid of Camille?

BUILDER. [*Staring at her, then dropping his glance*] Camille? What's she got to do with it?

MRS. BUILDER. I thought perhaps you found *her* irritating.

BUILDER. Why should I?

CAMILLE comes in from the dining-room with the coffee.

Put it there. I want some brandy, please.

CAMILLE. I bring it, Monsieur.

[*She goes back demurely into the dining-room.*

BUILDER. Topping's got toothache, poor chap! [*Pouring out the coffee*] Can't you suggest any way of making Athene see reason? Think of the example! Maud will be kicking over next. I shan't be able to hold my head up here.

MRS. BUILDER. I'm afraid I can't do that for you.

BUILDER. [*Exasperated*] Look here, Julia! That wretched girl said something to me about our life together. What—what's the matter with that?

MRS. BUILDER. It is irritating.

BUILDER. Be explicit.

MRS. BUILDER. We have lived together twenty-three years, John. No talk will change such things.

BUILDER. Is it a question of money? You can always have more. You know that. [MRS. BUILDER *smiles*] Oh! don't smile like that; it makes me feel quite sick!

CAMILLE enters with a decanter and little glasses, from the dining-room.

CAMILLE. The brandy, sir. Monsieur Ralph Builder has just come.

MRS. BUILDER. Ask him in, Camille.

CAMILLE. Yes, Madame.

[*She goes through the doorway into the hall.* MRS. BUILDER, *following towards the door, meets* RALPH BUILDER, *a man rather older than* BUILDER *and of opposite build and manner. He has a pleasant, whimsical face and grizzled hair.*

MRS. BUILDER. John wants to consult you, Ralph.

RALPH. That's very gratifying.

She passes him and goes out, leaving the two brothers eying one another.

About the Welsh contract?

BUILDER. No. Fact is, Ralph, something very horrible's happened.

RALPH. Athene gone and got married?

BUILDER. No. It's—it's that she's gone and—and not got married.

[RALPH *utters a sympathetic whistle.*

Jolly, isn't it?

RALPH. To whom?

BUILDER. A young flying bounder.

RALPH. And why?

BUILDER. Some crazy rubbish about family life, of all things.

RALPH. Athene's a most interesting girl. All these young people are so queer and delightful.

BUILDER. By George, Ralph, you may thank your stars you haven't got a delightful daughter. Yours are good, decent girls.

RALPH. Athene's tremendously good and decent, John. I'd bet any money she's doing this on the highest principles.

BUILDER. Behaving like a——

RALPH. Don't say what you'll regret, old man! Athene always took things seriously—bless her!

BUILDER. Julia thinks you might help. You never seem to have any domestic troubles.

RALPH. No-o. I don't think we do.

BUILDER. How d'you account for it?

RALPH. I must ask at home.

BUILDER. Dash it! You must know!

RALPH. We're all fond of each other.

BUILDER. Well, I'm fond of my girls too; I suppose I'm not amiable enough. H'm?

RALPH. Well, old man, you do get blood to the head. But what's Athene's point, exactly?

BUILDER. Family life isn't idyllic, so she thinks she and the young man oughtn't to have one.

RALPH. I see. Home experience?

BUILDER. Hang it all, a family's a family! There must be a head.

RALPH. But no tail, old chap.

BUILDER. You don't let your women folk do just as they like?

RALPH. Always.

BUILDER. What happens if one of your girls wants to do an improper thing? [RALPH *shrugs his shoulders*] You don't stop her?

RALPH. Do you?

BUILDER. I try to.

RALPH. Exactly. And she does it. I don't and she doesn't.

BUILDER. [*With a short laugh*] Good Lord! I suppose you'd have me eat humble pie and tell Athene she can go on living in sin and offending society, and have my blessing to round it off.

RALPH. I think if you did she'd probably marry him.

BUILDER. You've never tested your theory, I'll bet.

RALPH. Not yet.

BUILDER. There you are.

RALPH. The *suaviter in modo* pays, John. The times are not what they were.

BUILDER. Look here! I want to get to the bottom of this. Do you tell me I'm any stricter than nine out of ten men?

RALPH. Only in practice.

BUILDER. [*Puzzled*] How do you mean?

RALPH. Well, you profess the principles of liberty, but you practise the principles of government.

BUILDER. H'm! [*Taking up the decanter*] Have some?

RALPH. No, thank you.

[BUILDER *fills and raises his glass.*

CAMILLE. [*Entering*] Madame left her coffee.

She comes forward, holds out a cup for BUILDER *to pour into, takes it and goes out.* BUILDER'S *glass remains suspended. He drinks the brandy off as she shuts the door.*

BUILDER. Life isn't all roses, Ralph.

RALPH. Sorry, old man.

BUILDER. I sometimes think I try myself too high. Well, about that Welsh contract?

RALPH. Let's take it.

BUILDER. If you'll attend to it. Frankly, I'm too upset.

As they go towards the door into the hall, MAUD *comes in from the dining-room, in hat and coat.*

RALPH. [*Catching sight of her*] Hallo! All well in your cosmogony, Maud?

MAUD. What is a cosmogony, Uncle?

RALPH. My dear, I—I don't know.

He goes out, followed by BUILDER. MAUD *goes quickly to the table, sits down and rests her elbows on it, her chin on her hands, looking at the door.*

BUILDER. [*Re-entering*] Well, Maud. You'd have won your bet!

MAUD. Oh! father, I—I've got some news for you.

BUILDER. [*Staring at her*] News—what?

MAUD. I'm awfully sorry, but I—I've got a job.

BUILDER. Now, don't go saying you're going in for Art, too, because I won't have it.

MAUD. Art? Oh! no! It's the—— [*With a jerk*] the Movies.

BUILDER, *who has taken up a pipe to fill, puts it down.*

BUILDER. [*Impressively*] I'm not in a joking mood.

MAUD. I'm not joking, father.

BUILDER. Then what are you talking about?

MAUD. You see, I—I've got a film face, and——

BUILDER. You've what? [*Going up to his daughter, he takes hold of her chin*] Don't talk nonsense! Your sister has just tried me to the limit.

MAUD. [*Removing his hand from her chin*] Don't oppose it, father, please! I've always wanted to earn my own living.

BUILDER. Living! Living!

MAUD. [*Gathering determination*] You can't stop me, father, because I shan't need support. I've got quite good terms.

BUILDER. [*Almost choking, but mastering himself.*] Do you mean to say you've gone as far as that?

MAUD. Yes. It's all settled.

BUILDER. Who put you up to this?

MAUD. No one. I've been meaning to, ever so long. I'm twenty-one, you know.

BUILDER. A film face! Good God! Now, look here! I will not have a daughter of mine mixed up with the stage. I've spent goodness knows what on your education—both of you.

MAUD. I don't want to be ungrateful; but I—I can't go on living at home.

BUILDER. You can't——! Why? You've every indulgence.

MAUD. [*Clearly and coldly*] I can remember occasions when your indulgence hurt, father. [*She wriggles her shoulders and back*] We never forgot or forgave that.

BUILDER. [*Uneasily*] That! You were just kids.

MAUD. Perhaps you'd like to begin again?

BUILDER. Don't twist my tail, Maud. I had the most painful scene with Athene this morning. Now come! Give up this silly notion! It's really too childish!

MAUD. [*Looking at him curiously*] I've heard you say ever so many times that no man was any good who couldn't make his own way, father. Well, women are the same as men, now. It's the law of the country. I only want to make my own way.

BUILDER. [*Trying to subdue his anger*] Now, Maud, don't be foolish. Consider my position here—a Town Councillor, a Magistrate, and Mayor next year. With one daughter living with a man she isn't married to——

MAUD. [*With lively interest*] Oh! So you did catch them out?

BUILDER. D'you mean to say you knew?

MAUD. Of course.

BUILDER. My God! I thought we were a Christian family.

MAUD. Oh! father.

BUILDER. Don't sneer at Christianity!

MAUD. There's only one thing wrong with Christians—they aren't!

BUILDER seizes her by the shoulders and shakes her vigorously. When he drops her shoulders, she gets up, gives him a vicious look, and suddenly stamps her foot on his toe with all her might.

BUILDER. [*With a yowl of pain*] You little devil!

MAUD. [*Who has put the table between them*] I won't stand being shaken.

BUILDER. [*Staring at her across the table*] You've got my temper up and you'll take the consequences. I'll make you toe the line.

MAUD. If you knew what a Prussian expression you've got!

BUILDER *passes his hand across his face uneasily, as if to wipe something off.*

No! It's too deep!

BUILDER. Are you my daughter or are you not?

MAUD. I certainly never wanted to be. I've always disliked you, father, ever since I was so high. I've seen through you. Do you remember when you used to come into the nursery because Jenny was pretty? You think we didn't notice that, but we did. And in the schoolroom—Miss Tipton. And d'you remember knocking our heads together? No, you don't; but we do. And——

BUILDER. You disrespectful monkey! Will you be quiet?

MAUD. No; you've got to hear things. You don't really love anybody but yourself, father. What's good for you has to be good for everybody. I've often heard you talk about independence, but it's a limited company and you've got all the shares.

BUILDER. Rot; only people who can support themselves have a right to independence.

MAUD. That's why you don't want me to support myself.

BUILDER. You can't! Film, indeed! You'd be in the gutter in a year. Athene's got her pittance, but you—you've got nothing.

MAUD. Except my face.

BUILDER. It's the face that brings women to ruin, my girl.

MAUD. Well, when I'm there I won't come to you to rescue me.

BUILDER. Now, mind—if you leave my house, I've done with you.

MAUD. I'd rather scrub floors now, than stay.

BUILDER. [*Almost pathetically*] Well, I'm damned! Look here, Maud—all this has been temper. You got my monkey up. I'm sorry I shook you; you've had your revenge on my toes. Now, come! Don't make things worse for me than they are. You've all the liberty you can reasonably want till you marry.

MAUD. He can't see it—he absolutely can't!

BUILDER. See what?

MAUD. That I want to live a life of my own.

He edges nearer to her, and she edges to keep her distance.

BUILDER. I don't know what's bitten you.

MAUD. The microbe of freedom; it's in the air.

BUILDER. Yes, and there it'll stay—that's the first sensible word you've uttered. Now, come! Take your hat off, and let's be friends!

MAUD *looks at him and slowly takes off her hat.*

BUILDER. [*Relaxing his attitude, with a sigh of relief*] That's right! [*Crosses to fireplace*].

MAUD. [*Springing to the door leading to the hall*] Good-bye, father!

BUILDER. [*Following her*] Monkey!

At the sound of a bolt shot, BUILDER *goes up to the window. There is a fumbling at the door, and* CAMILLE *appears.*

BUILDER. What's the matter with that door?

CAMILLE. It was bolted, Monsieur.

BUILDER. Who bolted it?

CAMILLE. [*Shrugging her shoulders*] I can't tell, Monsieur. [*She collects the cups, and halts close to him. Softly*] Monsieur is not 'appy.

BUILDER. [*Surprised*] What? No! Who'd be happy in a household like mine?

CAMILLE. But so strong a man—I wish *I* was a strong man, not a weak woman.

BUILDER. [*Regarding her with reluctant admiration*] Why, what's the matter with *you?*

CAMILLE. Will Monsieur have another glass of brandy before I take it?

BUILDER. No! Yes—I will.

She pours it out, and he drinks it, hands her the glass and sits down suddenly in an armchair. CAMILLE *puts the glass on a tray, and looks for a box of matches from the mantelshelf.*

CAMILLE. A light, Monsieur?

BUILDER. Please.

CAMILLE. [*She trips over his feet and sinks on to his knee*] Oh! Monsieur!

BUILDER *flames up and catches her in his arms.*

Oh! Monsieur!

BUILDER. You little devil!

She suddenly kisses him, and he returns the kiss. While they are engaged in this entrancing occupation, MRS. BUILDER *opens the door from the hall, watches unseen for a few seconds, and quietly goes out again.*

BUILDER. [*Pushing her back from him, whether at the sound of the door or of a still small voice*] What am I doing?

CAMILLE. Kissing.

BUILDER. I—I forgot myself. [*They rise.*

CAMILLE. It was na-ice.

BUILDER. I didn't mean to. You go away—go away!

CAMILLE. Oh! Monsieur, that spoil it.

BUILDER. [*Regarding her fixedly*] It's my opinion you're a temptation of the devil. You know you sat down on purpose.

CAMILLE. Well, perhaps.

BUILDER. What business had you to? I'm a family man.

CAMILLE. Yes. What a pity! But does it matter?

BUILDER. [*Much beset*] Look here, you know! This won't do! It won't do! I—I've got my reputation to think of!

CAMILLE. So 'ave I! But there is lots of time to think of it in between.

BUILDER. I knew you were dangerous. I always knew it.

CAMILLE. What a thing to say of a little woman!

BUILDER. We're not in Paris.

CAMILLE. [*Clasping her hands*] Oh! 'Ow I wish we was!

BUILDER. Look here—I can't stand this; you've got to go. Out with you! I've always kept a firm hand on myself, and I'm not going to——

CAMILLE. But I admire you so!

BUILDER. Suppose my wife had come in?

CAMILLE. Oh! Don't suppose any such a disagreeable thing! If you were not so strict, you would feel much 'appier.

BUILDER. [*Staring at her*] You're a temptress!

CAMILLE. I lofe pleasure, and I don't get any. And you 'ave such a duty, you don't get any sport. Well, I am 'ere!

She stretches herself, and BUILDER *utters a deep sound.*

BUILDER. [*On the edge of succumbing*] It's all against my—I won't do it! It's—it's wrong!

CAMILLE. Oh! La, la!

BUILDER. [*Suddenly revolting*] No! If you thought it a sin—I—might. But you don't; you're nothing but a—a little heathen.

CAMILLE. Why should it be better if I thought it a sin?

BUILDER. Then—then I should know where I was. As it is——

CAMILLE. The English 'ave no idea of pleasure. They make it all so coarse and virtuous.

BUILDER. Now, out you go before I——! Go on!

He goes over to the door and opens it. His wife is outside in a hat and coat. She comes in.

[*Stammering*] Oh! Here you are—I wanted you.

CAMILLE, *taking up the tray, goes out Left, swinging her hips a very little.*

BUILDER. Going out?

MRS. BUILDER. Obviously.

BUILDER. Where?

MRS. BUILDER. I don't know at present.

BUILDER. I wanted to talk to you about—Maud.

MRS. BUILDER. It must wait.

BUILDER. She's—she's actually gone and——

MRS. BUILDER. I must tell you that I happened to look in a minute ago.

BUILDER. [*In absolute dismay*] You! You what?

MRS. BUILDER. Yes. I will put no obstacle in the way of your pleasures.

BUILDER. [*Aghast*] Put no obstacle? What do you mean? Julia, how can you say a thing like that? Why, I've only just——

MRS. BUILDER. Don't! I saw.

BUILDER. The girl *fell* on my knees. Julia, she did. She's—she's a little devil. I—I resisted her. I give you my word there's been nothing beyond a kiss, under great provocation. I—I apologise.

MRS. BUILDER. [*Bows her head*] Thank you! I quite understand. But you must forgive my feeling it impossible to remain a wet blanket any longer.

BUILDER. What! Because of a little thing like that—all over in two minutes, and I doing my utmost.

MRS. BUILDER. My dear John, the fact that you had to do your utmost is quite enough. I feel continually humiliated in your house, and I want to leave it—quite quietly, without fuss of any kind.

BUILDER. But—my God! Julia, this is awful—it's absurd! How can you? I'm your husband. Really—your saying you don't mind what I do—it's not right; it's immoral!

MRS. BUILDER. I'm afraid you don't see what goes on in those who live with you. So, I'll just go. Don't bother!

BUILDER. Now, look here, Julia, you can't mean this seriously. You can't! Think of my position! You've never set yourself up against me before.

MRS. BUILDER. But I do now.

BUILDER. [*After staring at her*] I've given you no real reason. I'll send the girl away. You ought to thank me for resisting a temptation that most men would have yielded to. After twenty-three years of married life, to kick up like this—you ought to be ashamed of yourself.

MRS. BUILDER. I'm sure you must think so.

BUILDER. Oh! for heaven's sake don't be sarcastic! You're my wife, and there's an end of it; you've no legal excuse. Don't be absurd!

MRS. BUILDER. Good-bye!

BUILDER. D'you realise that you're encouraging me to go wrong? That's a pretty thing for a wife to do. You ought to keep your husband straight.

MRS. BUILDER. How beautifully put!

BUILDER. [*Almost pathetically*] Don't rile me, Julia! I've had an awful day. First Athene—then Maud—then that girl—and now you! All at once like this! Like a swarm of bees about one's head. [*Pleading*] Come, now, Julia, don't be so—so impracticable! You'll make us the laughing-stock of the whole town. A man in my position, and can't keep his own family; it's preposterous!

MRS. BUILDER. Your own family have lives and thoughts and feelings of their own.

BUILDER. Oh! This damned Woman's business! I knew how it would be when we gave you the vote. You and I are married, and our daughters are our daughters. Come, Julia. Where's your common-sense? After twenty-three years! You know I can't do without you!

MRS. BUILDER. You could—quite easily. You can tell people what you like.

BUILDER. My God! I never heard anything so immoral in all my life from the mother of two grown-up girls. No wonder they've turned out as they have! What is it you want, for goodness sake?

MRS. BUILDER. We just want to be away from you, that's all. I assure you it's best. When you've shown some consideration for our feelings and some real sign that we exist apart from you—we could be friends again—perhaps—I don't know.

BUILDER. Friends! Good heavens! With one's own wife and daughters! [*With great earnestness*] Now, look here, Julia, you haven't lived with me all this time without knowing that I'm a man of strong passions; I've been a faithful husband to you—yes, I have. And that means resisting all sorts of temptations you know nothing of. If you withdraw from my society I won't answer for the consequences. In fact, I can't have you withdrawing. I'm not going to see myself going to the devil and losing the good opinion of everybody round me. A bargain's a bargain. And until I've broken my side of it, and I tell you I haven't—you've no business to break yours. That's flat. So now, put all that out of your head.

MRS. BUILDER. No.

BUILDER. [*Intently*] D'you realise that I've supported you in luxury and comfort?

MRS. BUILDER. I think I've earned it.

BUILDER. And how do you propose to live? *I* shan't give you a penny. Come, Julia, don't be such an idiot! Fancy letting a kiss which no man could have helped, upset you like this!

MRS. BUILDER. The Camille, and the last straw!

BUILDER. [*Sharply*] I won't have it. So now you know.

[*But* MRS. BUILDER *has very swiftly gone.*

Julia, I tell you—— [*The outer door is heard being closed*] Damnation! I will not have it! They're all mad! Here—where's my hat?

He looks distractedly round him, wrenches open the door, and a moment later the street door is heard to shut with a bang.

CURTAIN.

ACT III

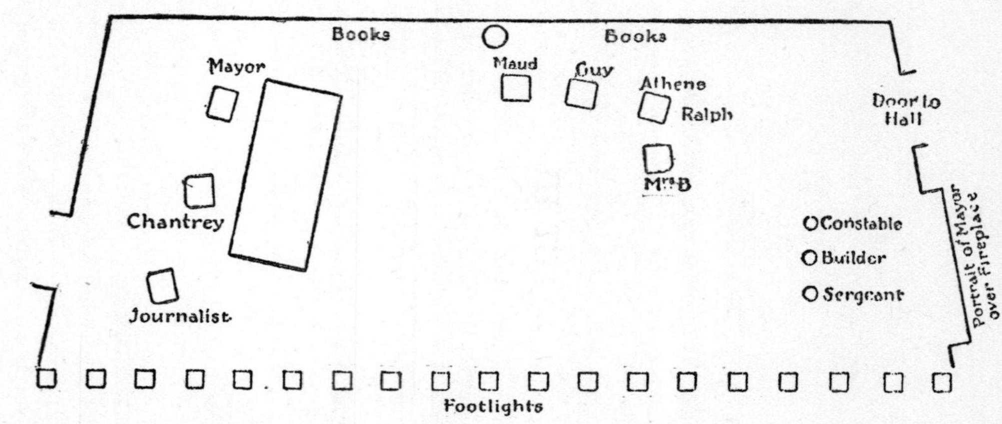
Books
Books
Mayor
Maud
Guy
Athene
Ralph
Door to Hall
Mrs B
Chantrey
Journalist
Constable
Builder
Sergeant
Portrait of Mayor over Fireplace
Footlights

ACT III

SCENE I

Ten o'clock the following morning, in the study of the Mayor of Breconridge, a panelled room with no window visible, a door Left back and a door Right forward. The entire back wall is furnished with books from floor to ceiling; the other walls are panelled and bare. Before the fireplace, Left, are two armchairs, and other chairs are against the walls. On the Right is a writing-bureau at right angles to the footlights, with a chair behind it. At its back corner stands HARRIS, *telephoning.*

HARRIS. What—[*Pause*] Well, it's infernally awkward, Sergeant. . . . The Mayor's in a regular stew. . . . [*Listens*] New constable? I should think so! Young fool! Look here, Martin, the only thing to do is to hear the charge *here* at once. I've sent for Mr. Chantrey; he's on his way. Bring Mr. Builder and the witnesses round sharp. See? And, I say, for God's sake keep it dark. Don't let the Press get on to it. Why you didn't let him go home——! Black eye? The constable? Well, serve him right. Blundering young ass! I mean, it's undermining all authority. . . . Well, you oughtn't—at least, I . . . Damn it all!—it's a nine days' wonder if it gets out——! All right! As soon as you can. [*He hangs up the receiver, puts a second chair behind the bureau, and other chairs facing it.*] [*To himself*] Here's a mess! Johnny BUILDER, of all men! What price Mayors!

[*The telephone rings.*

Hallo? . . . Poaching charge? Well, bring him too; only, I say, keep him back till the other's over. By the way, Mr. Chantrey's going shooting. He'll want to get off by eleven. What? . . . Righto!

As he hangs up the receiver the MAYOR *enters. He looks worried, and is still dressed with the indefinable wrongness of a burgher.*

MAYOR. Well, 'Arris?

HARRIS. They'll be over in five minutes, Mr. Mayor.

MAYOR. Mr. Chantrey?

HARRIS. On his way, sir.

MAYOR. I've had some awkward things to deal with in my time, 'Arris, but this is just about the [*Sniffs*] limit.

HARRIS. Most uncomfortable, sir; most uncomfortable!

MAYOR. Put a book on the chair, 'Arris; I like to sit 'igh.

HARRIS *puts a volume of Encyclopædia on the Mayor's chair behind the bureau.*

[*Deeply*] Our fellow-magistrate! A family man! In my shoes next year. I suppose he won't be, now. You can't keep these things dark.

HARRIS. I've warned Martin, sir, to use the utmost discretion. Here's Mr. Chantrey.

By the door Left, a pleasant and comely gentleman has entered, dressed with indefinable rightness in shooting clothes.

MAYOR. Ah, Chantrey!

CHANTREY. How de do, Mr. Mayor? [*Nodding to* HARRIS] This is extraordinarily unpleasant.

[*The* MAYOR *nods.*

What on earth's he been doing?

HARRIS. Assaulting one of his own daughters with a stick; and resisting the police.

CHANTREY. [*With a low whistle*] Daughter! Charity begins at home.

HARRIS. There's a black eye.

MAYOR. Whose?

HARRIS. The constable's.

CHANTREY. How did the police come into it?

HARRIS. I don't know, sir. The worst of it is he's been at the police station since four o'clock yesterday. The Superintendent's away, and Martin never will take responsibility.

CHANTREY. By George! he will be mad. John Builder's a choleric fellow.

MAYOR. [*Nodding*] He is. 'Ot temper, and an 'igh sense of duty.

HARRIS. There's one other charge, Mr. Mayor—poaching. I told them to keep that back till after.

CHANTREY. Oh, well, we'll make short work of that. I want to get off by eleven, Harris. I shall be late for the first drive anyway. John Builder! I say, Mayor—but for the grace of God, there go we!

MAYOR. Harris, go out and bring them in yourself; don't let the servants—— [HARRIS *goes out Left.*

The MAYOR *takes the upper chair behind the bureau, sitting rather higher because of the book than* CHANTREY, *who takes the lower. Now that they are in the seats of justice, a sort of reticence falls on them, as if they were afraid of giving away their attitudes of mind to some unseen presence.*

MAYOR. [*Suddenly*] H'm!

CHANTREY. Touch of frost. Birds ought to come well to the guns—no wind. I like these October days.

MAYOR. I think I 'ear them. H'm.

CHANTREY *drops his eyeglass and puts on a pair of "grandfather" spectacles. The* MAYOR *clears his throat and takes up a pen. They neither of them look up as the door is opened and a little procession files in. First* HARRIS; *then* RALPH BUILDER, ATHENE, HERRINGHAME, MAUD, MRS. BUILDER, SERGEANT MARTIN, *carrying a heavy Malacca cane with a silver knob;* JOHN BUILDER *and the* CONSTABLE MOON, *a young man with one black eye. No funeral was ever attended by mutes so solemn and dejected. They stand in a sort of row.*

MAYOR. [*Without looking up*] Sit down, ladies; sit down.

HARRIS *and* HERRINGHAME *succeed in placing the three women in chairs.* RALPH BUILDER *also sits.* HERRINGHAME *stands behind.* JOHN BUILDER *remains standing between the* TWO POLICEMEN. *His face is unshaved and menacing, but he stands erect staring straight at the* MAYOR. HARRIS *goes to the side of the bureau, Back, to take down the evidence.*

MAYOR. Charges!

SERGEANT. John Builder, of The Cornerways, Breconridge, Contractor and Justice of the Peace, charged with assaulting his daughter Maud Builder by striking her with a stick in the presence of Constable Moon and two other persons; also with resisting Constable Moon in the execution of his duty, and injuring his eye. Constable Moon!

MOON. [*Stepping forward—one, two—like an automaton, and saluting*] In River Road yesterday afternoon, Your Worship, about three-thirty p.m., I was attracted by a young woman callin' "Constable" outside a courtyard. On hearing the words "Follow me, quick," I followed her to a painter's studio inside the courtyard, where I found three persons in the act of disagreement. No sooner 'ad I appeared than the defendant, who was engaged in draggin' a woman towards the door, turns to the young woman who accompanied me, with violence. "You dare, father," she says; whereupon he hit her twice with the stick the same which is produced, in the presence of myself and the two other persons, which I'm given to understand is his wife and other daughter.

MAYOR. Yes; never mind what you're given to understand.

MOON. No, sir. The party struck turns to me and says, "Come in. I give this man in charge for assault." I moves accordingly with the words: "I saw you. Come along with me." The defendant turns to me sharp and says: "You stupid lout—I'm a magistrate." "Come off it," I says to the best of my recollection. "You struck this woman in my presence," I says, "and you come along!" We were then at close quarters. The defendant gave me a push with the words "Get out, you idiot!" "Not at all," I replies, and took 'old of his arm. A struggle ensues, in the course of which I receives the black eye which I herewith produce. [*He touches his eye with awful solemnity. The* MAYOR *clears his throat;* CHANTREY'S *eyes goggle;* HARRIS *bends over and writes rapidly.*

During the struggle, Your Worship, a young man has appeared on the scene, and at the instigation of the young woman, the same who was assaulted, assists me in securing the prisoner, whose language and resistance was violent in the extreme. We placed him in a cab which we found outside, and I conveyed him to the station.

CHANTREY. What was his—er—conduct in the—er—cab?

MOON. He sat quiet.

CHANTREY. That seems——

MOON. Seein' I had his further arm twisted behind him.

MAYOR. [*Looking at* BUILDER] Any questions to ask him?

BUILDER *makes not the faintest sign, and the* MAYOR *drops his glance.*

MAYOR. Sergeant?

MOON *steps back two paces, and the* SERGEANT *steps two paces forward.*

SERGEANT. At ten minutes to four, Your Worship, yesterday afternoon, Constable Moon brought the defendant to the station in a four-wheeled cab. On his recounting the circumstances of the assault, they were taken down and read over to the defendant with the usual warning. The defendant said nothing. In view of the double assault and the condition of the constable's eye, and in the absence of the Superintendent, I thought it my duty to retain the defendant for the night.

MAYOR. The defendant said nothing?

SERGEANT. He 'as not opened his lips to my knowledge, Your Worship, from that hour to this.

MAYOR. Any questions to ask the Sergeant?

BUILDER *continues to stare at the* MAYOR *without a word.*

MAYOR. Very well!

The MAYOR *and* CHANTREY *now consult each other inaudibly, and the* MAYOR *nods.*

MAYOR. Miss Maud Builder, will you tell us what you know of this—er—occourrence?

MAUD. [*Rising; with eyes turning here and there*] Must I?

MAYOR. I'm afraid you must.

MAUD. [*After a look at her father, who never turns his eyes from the* MAYOR'S *face*] I—I wish to withdraw the charge of striking me, please. I—I never meant to make it. I was in a temper—I saw red.

MAYOR. I see. A—a domestic disagreement. Very well, that charge is withdrawn. You do not appear to have been hurt, and that seems to me quite proper. Now, tell me what you know of the assault on the constable. Is his account correct?

MAUD. [*Timidly*] Ye-yes. Only——

MAYOR. Yes? Tell us the truth.

MAUD. [*Resolutely*] Only, I don't think my father hit the constable. I think the stick did that.

MAYOR. Oh, the stick? But—er—the stick was in 'is 'and, wasn't it?

MAUD. Yes; but I mean, my father saw red, and the constable saw red, and the stick flew up between them and hit him in the eye.

CHANTREY. And then he saw black?

MAYOR. [*With corrective severity*] But did 'e 'it 'im with the stick?

MAUD. No-no. I don't think he did.

MAYOR. Then who supplied the—er—momentum?

MAUD. I think there was a struggle for the cane, and it flew up.

MAYOR. Hand up the cane.

The SERGEANT *hands up the cane. The* MAYOR *and* CHANTREY *examine it.*

MAYOR. Which end—do you suggest—inflicted this injury?

MAUD. Oh! the knob end, sir.

MAYOR. What do you say to that, constable?

MOON. [*Stepping the mechanical two paces*] I don't deny there was a struggle, Your Worship, but it's my impression I was 'it.

CHANTREY. Of course you were hit; we can see that. But with the cane or with the fist?

MOON. [*A little flurried*] I—I—with the fist, sir.

MAYOR. Be careful. Will you swear to that?

MOON. [*With that sudden uncertainty which comes over the most honest in such circumstances*] Not—not so to speak in black and white, Your Worship; but that was my idea at the time.

MAYOR. You won't swear to it?

MOON. I'll swear he called me an idiot and a lout; the words made a deep impression on me.

CHANTREY. [*To himself*] *Mort aux vaches!*

MAYOR. Eh? That'll do, constable; stand back. Now, who else saw the struggle? Mrs. Builder. You're not obliged to say anything unless you like. That's your privilege as his wife.

While he is speaking the door has been opened, and HARRIS *has gone swiftly to it, spoken to someone and returned. He leans forward to the* MAYOR.

Eh? Wait a minute. Mrs. Builder, do you wish to give evidence?

MRS. BUILDER. [*Rising*] No, Mr. Mayor.

[MRS. BUILDER *sits.*

MAYOR. Very good. [*To* HARRIS] Now then, what is it?

HARRIS *says something in a low and concerned voice. The* MAYOR'S *face lengthens. He leans to his right and consults* CHANTREY, *who gives a faint and deprecating shrug. A moment's silence.*

MAYOR. This is an open Court. The Press have the right to attend if they wish.

HARRIS *goes to the door and admits a young man in glasses, of a pleasant C.3 appearance, and indicates to him a chair at the back. At this untimely happening* BUILDER'S *eyes have moved from side to side, but now he regains his intent and bull-like stare at his fellow-justices.*

MAYOR. [*To Maud*] You can sit down, Miss Builder.

[MAUD *resumes her seat.*

Miss Athene Builder, you were present, I think?

ATHENE. [*Rising*] Yes, sir.

MAYOR. What do you say to this matter?

ATHENE. I didn't see anything very clearly, but I think my sister's account is correct, sir.

MAYOR. Is it your impression that the cane inflicted the injury?

ATHENE. [*In a low voice*] Yes.

MAYOR. With or without deliberate intent?

ATHENE. Oh! without.

[BUILDER *looks at her.*

MAYOR. But you were not in a position to see very well?

ATHENE. No, sir.

MAYOR. Your sister having withdrawn her charge, we needn't go into that. Very good!

[*He motions her to sit down.*

ATHENE, *turning her eyes on her Father's impassive figure, sits.*

MAYOR. Now, there was a young man. [*Pointing to* HERRINGHAME] Is this the young man?

MOON. Yes, Your Worship.

MAYOR. What's your name?

GUY. Guy Herringhame.

MAYOR. Address?

GUY. Er—the Aerodrome, sir.

MAYOR. Private, I mean?

[*The moment is one of considerable tension.*

GUY. [*With an effort*] At the moment, sir, I haven't one. I've just left my diggings, and haven't yet got any others.

MAYOR. H'm! The Aerodrome. How did you come to be present?

GUY. I—er——

BUILDER'S *eyes go round and rest on him for a moment.*

It's in my sister's studio that Miss Athene Builder

is at present working, sir. I just happened to—to turn up.

MAYOR. Did you appear on the scene, as the constable says, during the struggle?

GUY. Yes, sir.

MAYOR. Did he summon you to his aid?

GUY. Ye—— No, sir. Miss Maud Builder did that.

MAYOR. What do you say to this blow?

GUY. [*Jerking his chin up a little*] Oh! I saw that clearly.

MAYOR. Well, let us hear.

GUY. The constable's arm struck the cane violently and it flew up and landed him in the eye.

MAYOR. [*With a little grunt*] You are sure of that?

GUY. Quite sure, sir.

MAYOR. Did you hear any language?

GUY. Nothing out of the ordinary, sir. One or two damns and blasts.

MAYOR. You call that ordinary?

GUY. Well, he's a—magistrate, sir.

The MAYOR *utters a profound grunt.* CHANTREY *smiles. There is a silence. Then the* MAYOR *leans over to* CHANTREY *for a short colloquy.*

CHANTREY. Did you witness any particular violence other than a resistance to arrest?

GUY. No, sir.

MAYOR. [*With a gesture of dismissal*] Very well. That seems to be the evidence. Defendant John Builder—what do you say to all this?

BUILDER. [*In a voice different from any we have heard from him*] Say! What business had he to touch me, a magistrate? I gave my daughter two taps with a cane in a private house, for interfering with me for taking my wife home——

MAYOR. That charge is not pressed, and we can't go into the circumstances. What do you wish to say about your conduct towards the constable?

BUILDER. [*In his throat*] Not a damned thing!

MAYOR. [*Embarrassed*] I—I didn't catch.

CHANTREY. Nothing—nothing, he said, Mr. Mayor.

MAYOR. [*Clearing his throat*] I understand, then, that you do not wish to h'offer any explanation?

BUILDER. I consider myself abominably treated, and I refuse to say another word.

MAYOR. [*Drily*] Very good. Miss Maud Builder.

[MAUD *stands up.*

MAYOR. When you spoke of the defendant seeing ed, what exactly did you mean?

MAUD. I mean that my father was so angry that e didn't know what he was doing.

CHANTREY. Would you say as angry as he—er—is now?

MAUD. [*With a faint smile*] Oh! much more angry.

[RALPH BUILDER *stands up.*

RALPH. Would you allow me to say a word, Mr. Mayor?

MAYOR. Speaking of your own knowledge, Mr. Builder?

RALPH. In regard to the state of my brother's

mind—yes, Mr. Mayor. He was undoubtedly under great strain yesterday; certain circumstances, domestic and otherwise——

MAYOR. You mean that he might have been, as one might say, beside himself?

RALPH. Exactly, sir.

MAYOR. Had you seen your brother?

RALPH. I had seen him shortly before this unhappy business.

The MAYOR *nods and makes a gesture, so that* MAUD *and* RALPH *sit down; then, leaning over, he confers in a low voice with* CHANTREY. *The rest all sit or stand exactly as if each was the only person in the room, except the* JOURNALIST, *who is writing busily and rather obviously making a sketch of* BUILDER.

MAYOR. Miss Athene Builder.

[ATHENE *stands up.*

This young man, Mr. Herringhame, I take it, is a friend of the family's? [*A moment of some tension.*

ATHENE. N-no, Mr. Mayor, not of my father or mother.

CHANTREY. An acquaintance of yours?

ATHENE. Yes.

MAYOR. Very good. [*He clears his throat*] As the defendant, wrongly, we think, refuses to offer his explanation of this matter, the Bench has to decide on the h'evidence as given. There seems to be some discrepancy as to the blow which the constable undoubtedly received. In view of this, we incline to take the testimony of Mr.——

[HARRIS *prompts him.*

Mr. 'Erringhame—as the party least inplicated personally in the affair, and most likely to 'ave a cool and impartial view. That evidence is to the effect that the blow was accidental. There is no doubt, however, that the defendant used reprehensible language, and offered some resistance to the constable in the execution of his duty. Evidence 'as been offered that he was in an excited state of mind; and it is possible—I don't say that this is any palliation—but it is possible that he may have thought his position as magistrate made him—er——

CHANTREY. [*Prompting*] Cæsar's wife.

MAYOR. Eh? We think, considering all the circumstances, and the fact that he has spent a night in a cell, that justice will be met by—er—discharging him with a caution.

BUILDER. [*With a deeply muttered*] The devil you do!

Walks out of the room. The JOURNALIST, *grabbing his pad, starts up and follows. The* BUILDERS *rise and huddle, and, with* HERRINGHAME, *are ushered out by* HARRIS.

MAYOR. [*Pulling out a large handkerchief and wiping his forehead*] My Aunt!

CHANTREY. These new constables, Mayor! I say, Builder'll have to go! Damn the Press, how they nose everything out! The Great Unpaid!—We shall get it again! [*He suddenly goes off into a fit of laughter*]

"Come off it," I says, "to the best of my recollection." Oh! Oh! I shan't hit a bird all day! That poor devil Builder! It's no joke for him. You did it well, Mayor; you did it well. British justice is safe in your hands. He blacked the fellow's eye all right. "Which I herewith produce." Oh! my golly! It beats the band!

His uncontrollable laughter and the MAYOR'S *rueful appreciation are exchanged with lightning rapidity for a preternatural solemnity, as the door opens, admitting* SERGEANT MARTIN *and the lugubrious object of their next attentions.*

MAYOR. Charges.

SERGEANT *steps forward to read the charge as*

The CURTAIN *falls.*

SCENE II

Noon the same day.

BUILDER'S study. TOPPING *is standing by the open window, looking up and down the street. A newspaper boy's voice is heard calling the first edition of his wares. It approaches from the Right.*

TOPPING. Here!

BOY'S VOICE. Right, guv'nor! Johnny Builder up before the beaks!

[*A paper is pushed up.*

TOPPING. [*Extending a penny*] What's that you're sayin'? You take care!

BOY'S VOICE. It's all 'ere. Johnny Builder—beatin' his wife! Dischawged.

TOPPING. Stop it, you young limb!

BOY'S VOICE. 'Allo! What's the matter wiv you? Why, it's Johnny Builder's house! [*Gives a cat-call*] 'Ere, buy anuvver! 'E'll want to read about 'isself. [*Appealing*] Buy anuvver, guv'nor!

TOPPING. Move on!

He retreats from the window, opening the paper.

BOY'S VOICE. [*Receding*] Payper! First edition! J.P. chawged! Payper!

TOPPING. [*To himself as he reads*] Crimes! Phew! That accounts for them bein' away all night.

While he is reading, CAMILLE *enters from the hall.*

Here! Have you seen this, Camel—in the Stop Press?

CAMILLE. No.

[*They read eagerly side by side.*

TOPPING. [*Finishing aloud*] "Tried to prevent her father from forcing her mother to return home with him, and he struck her for so doing. She did not press the charge. The arrested gentleman, who said he acted under great provocation, was discharged with a caution." Well, I'm blowed! He has gone and done it!

CAMILLE. A black eye!

TOPPING. [*Gazing at her*] Have you had any hand in this? I've seen you making *your* lovely black eyes at him. You foreigners—you're a loose lot!

CAMILLE. You are drunk!

TOPPING. Not yet, my dear. [*Reverting to the paper; philosophically*] Well, this little lot's bust up! The favourites will fall down. Johnny Builder! Who'd have thought it?

CAMILLE. He is an obstinate man.

TOPPING. Ah! He's right up against it now. Comes of not knowin' when to stop bein' firm. If you meet a wall with your 'ead, it's any odds on the wall, Camel. Though, if you listened to some, you wouldn't think it. What'll he do now, I wonder? Any news of the mistress?

CAMILLE. [*Shaking her head*] I have pack her tr-runks.

TOPPING. Why?

CAMILLE. Because she take her jewels yesterday.

TOPPING. Deuce she did! They generally leave 'em. Take back yer gifts! She throws the baubles at 'is 'ead. [*Again staring at her*] You're a deep one, you know!

[*There is the sound of a cab stopping.*

Wonder if that's him! [*He goes towards the hall.*

CAMILLE *watchfully shifts towards the dining-room door.* MAUD *enters.*

MAUD. Is my father back, Topping?

TOPPING. Not yet, Miss.

MAUD. I've come for mother's things.

CAMILLE. They are r-ready.

MAUD. [*Eyeing her*] Topping, get them down, please.

TOPPING, *after a look at them both, goes out into the hall.*

Very clever of you to have got them ready.

CAMILLE. I am clevare.

MAUD. [*Almost to herself*] Yes—father may, and he may not.

CAMILLE. Look! If you think I am a designing woman, you are mistook. I know when things are too 'ot. I am not sorry to go.

MAUD. Oh! you are going?

CAMILLE. Yes, I am going. How can I stay when there is no lady in the 'ouse?

MAUD. Not even if you're asked to?

CAMILLE. Who will ask me?

MAUD. That we shall see.

CAMILLE. Well, you will see I have an opinion of my own.

MAUD. Oh! yes, you're clear-headed enough.

CAMILLE. I am not arguing. Good-morning!

[*Exits up Left.*

MAUD *regards her stolidly as she goes out into the dining-room, then takes up the paper and reads.*

MAUD. Horrible!

[TOPPING *re-enters from the hall.*

TOPPING. I've got 'em on the cab, Miss. I didn't put your ten bob on yesterday, because the animal finished last. You can't depend on horses.

MAUD. [*Touching the newspaper*] This is a frightful business, Topping.

TOPPING. Ah! However did it happen, Miss Maud?

MAUD. [*Tapping the newspaper*] It's all true. He came after my mother to Miss Athene's, and I—I couldn't stand it. I did what it says here; and now I'm sorry. Mother's dreadfully upset. You know father as well as anyone, Topping; what do you think he'll do now?

TOPPING. [*Sucking in his cheeks*] Well, you see, Miss, it's like this: Up to now Mr. Builder's always had the respect of everybody——

[MAUD *moves her head impatiently.*

outside his own house, of course. Well, now he hasn't got it. Pishchologically that's bound to touch him.

MAUD. Of course; but which way? Will he throw up the sponge, or try and stick it out here?

TOPPING. He won't throw up the sponge, Miss; more likely to squeeze it down the back of their necks.

MAUD. He'll be asked to resign, of course.

The NEWSPAPER BOY'S VOICE *is heard again approaching: "First edition! Great sensation! Local magistrate before the Bench! Pay-per!"*

Oh, dear! I wish I hadn't! But I couldn't see mother being——

TOPPING. Don't you fret, Miss; he'll come through. His jaw's above his brow, as you might say.

MAUD. What?

TOPPING. [*Nodding*] Phreenology, Miss. I rather follow that. When the jaw's big and the brow is small, it's a sign of character. I always think the master might have been a Scotchman, except for his fishionomy.

MAUD. A Scotsman?

TOPPING. So down on anything soft, Miss. Haven't you noticed whenever one of these 'Umanitarians writes to the papers, there's always a Scotchman after him next morning. Seems to be a fact of 'uman nature, like introducin' rabbits into a new country and then weasels to get rid of 'em. And then something to keep down the weasels. But *I* never can see what could keep down a Scotchman! You seem to reach the hapex there!

MAUD. Miss Athene was married this morning, Topping. We've just come from the Registrar's.

TOPPING. [*Immovably*] Indeed, Miss. I thought perhaps she was about to be.

MAUD. Oh!

TOPPING. Comin' events. I saw the shadder yesterday.

MAUD. Well, it's all right. She's coming on here with my uncle.

[*A cab is heard driving up.*

That's them, I expect. We all feel awful about father.

TOPPING. Ah! I shouldn't be surprised if he feels awful about you, Miss.

MAUD. [*At the window*] It *is* them.

TOPPING *goes out into the hall;* ATHENE *and* RALPH *enter Right.*

MAUD. Where's father, Uncle Ralph?

RALPH. With his solicitor.

ATHENE. We left Guy with mother at the studio. She still thinks she ought to come. She keeps on saying she *must*, now father's in a hole.

MAUD. I've got her things on the cab; she ought to be perfectly free to choose.

RALPH. You've got freedom on the brain, Maud.

MAUD. So would you, Uncle Ralph, if you had father about.

RALPH. I'm his partner, my dear.

MAUD. Yes; how *do* you manage him?

RALPH. I've never yet given him in charge.

ATHENE. What *do* you do, Uncle Ralph?

RALPH. Undermine him when I can.

MAUD. And when you can't?

RALPH. Undermine the other fellow. You can't go to those movie people now, Maud. They'd star you as the celebrated Maud Builder who gave her father into custody. Come to us instead, and have perfect freedom, till all this blows over.

MAUD. Oh! what will father be like now?

ATHENE. It's so queer you and he being brothers, Uncle Ralph.

RALPH. There are two sides to every coin, my dear. John's the head—and I'm the tail. He has the sterling qualities. Now, you girls have got to smooth him down, and make up to him. You've tried him pretty high.

MAUD. [*Stubbornly*] I never wanted him for a father, Uncle.

RALPH. They do wonderful things nowadays with inherited trouble. Come, are you going to be nice to him, both of you?

ATHENE. We're going to try.

RALPH. Good! I don't even now understand how it happened.

MAUD. When you went out with Guy, it wasn't three minutes before he came. Mother had just told us about—well, about something beastly. Father wanted us to go, and we agreed to go out for five minutes while he talked to mother. We went, and when we came back he told me to get a cab to take mother home. Poor mother stood there looking like a ghost, and he began hunting and hauling her towards the door. I saw red, and instead of a cab I fetched that policeman. Of course father did black his eye. Guy was splendid.

ATHENE. You gave him the lead.

MAUD. I couldn't help it, seeing father standing there all dumb.

ATHENE. It was awful! Uncle, why didn't you come back with Guy?

MAUD. Oh, yes! why didn't you, Uncle?

ATHENE. When Maud had gone for the cab, I warned him not to use force. I told him it was against the law, but he only said: "The law be damned!"

RALPH. Well, it all sounds pretty undignified.

MAUD. Yes; everybody saw red.

They have not seen the door opened from the hall, and BUILDER *standing there. He is still unshaven, a little sunken in the face, with a glum, glowering expression. He has a document in his hand. He advances a step or two and they see him.*

ATHENE and MAUD. [*Aghast*] Father!

BUILDER. Ralph, oblige me! See them off the premises!

RALPH. Steady, John!

BUILDER. Go!

MAUD. [*Proudly*] All right! We thought you might like to know that Athene's married, and that I've given up the movies. Now we'll go.

BUILDER *turns his back on them, and, sitting down at his writing-table, writes.*

After a moment's whispered conversation with their Uncle, the two girls go out.

RALPH BUILDER *stands gazing with whimsical commiseration at his brother's back. As* BUILDER *finishes writing, he goes up and puts his hand on his brother's shoulder.*

RALPH. This is an awful jar, old man!

BUILDER. Here's what I've said to that fellow:—

"MR. MAYOR,—You had the effrontery to-day to discharge me *with a caution*—forsooth!—your fellow-magistrate. I've consulted my solicitor as to whether an action will lie for false imprisonment. I'm informed that it won't. I take this opportunity of saying that justice in this town is a travesty. I have no wish to be associated further with you or your fellows; but you are vastly mistaken if you imagine that I shall resign my position on the Bench or the Town Council.—Yours,

"JOHN BUILDER."

RALPH. I say—keep your sense of humour, old boy.

BUILDER. [*Grimly*] Humour? I've spent a night in a cell. See this! [*He holds out the document*] It disinherits my family.

RALPH. John!

BUILDER. I've done with those two ladies. As to my wife—if she doesn't come back——! When I suffer, I make others suffer.

RALPH. Julia's very upset, my dear fellow; we all are. The girls came here to try and——

BUILDER. [*Rising*] They may go to hell! If that lousy Mayor thinks I'm done with—he's mistaken! [*He rings the bell*] I don't want any soft sawder. I'm a fighter.

RALPH. [*In a low voice*] The enemy stands within the gate, old chap.

BUILDER. What's that?

RALPH. Let's boss our own natures before we boss those of other people. Have a sleep on it, John, before you do anything.

BUILDER. Sleep? I hadn't a wink last night. If you'd passed the night I had——

RALPH. I hadn't many myself.

[TOPPING *enters.*

BUILDER. Take this note to the Mayor with my compliments, and don't bring back an answer.

TOPPING. Very good, sir. There's a gentleman from the "Comet" in the hall, sir. Would you see him for a minute, he says.

BUILDER. Tell him to go to——

A voice says, "Mr. Builder!" BUILDER *turns*

to see the figure of the JOURNALIST *in the hall doorway.* TOPPING *goes out.*

JOURNALIST. [*Advancing with his card*] Mr. Builder, it's very good of you to see me. I had the pleasure this morning—I mean—I tried to reach you when you left the Mayor's. I thought you would probably have your own side of this unfortunate matter. We shall be glad to give it every prominence.

TOPPING *has withdrawn, and* RALPH BUILDER, *at the window, stands listening.*

BUILDER. [*Drily, regarding the* JOURNALIST, *who has spoken in a pleasant and polite voice*] Very good of you!

JOURNALIST. Not at all, sir. We felt that you would almost certainly have good reasons of your own which would put the matter in quite a different light.

BUILDER. Good reasons? I should think so! I tell you—a very little more of this liberty—licence I call it—and there isn't a man who'll be able to call himself head of a family.

JOURNALIST. [*Encouragingly*] Quite!

BUILDER. If the law thinks it can back up revolt, it's damned well mistaken. I struck my daughter—I was in a passion, as *you* would have been.

JOURNALIST. [*Encouraging*] I'm sure——

BUILDER. [*Glaring at him*] Well, I don't know that you would; you look a soft sort; but any man with any blood in him.

JOURNALIST. Can one ask what she was doing, sir? We couldn't get that point quite clear.

BUILDER. Doing? I just had my arm round my wife, trying to induce her to come home with me after a little family tiff, and this girl came at me. I lost my temper, and tapped her with my cane. And—that policeman brought by my own daughter—a policeman! If the law is going to enter private houses and abrogate domestic authority, where the hell shall we be?

JOURNALIST. [*Encouraging*] No, I'm sure—I'm sure!

BUILDER. The maudlin sentimentality in these days is absolutely rotting this country. A man can't be master in his own house, can't require his wife to fulfil her duties, can't attempt to control the conduct of his daughters, without coming up against it and incurring odium. A man can't control his employees; he can't put his foot down on rebellion anywhere, without a lot of humanitarians and licence-lovers howling at him.

JOURNALIST. Excellent, sir; excellent!

BUILDER. Excellent? It's damnable. Here am I—a man who's always tried to do his duty in private life and public—brought up before the Bench—my God! because I was doing that duty; with a little too much zeal, perhaps—I'm not an angel!

JOURNALIST. No! No! of course.

BUILDER. A proper Englishman never is. But there are no proper Englishmen nowadays.

[*He crosses the room in his fervour.*

RALPH. [*Suddenly*] As I look at faces——

BUILDER. [*Absorbed*] What! I told this young man I wasn't an angel.

JOURNALIST. [*Drawing him on*] Yes, sir; I quite understand.

BUILDER. If the law thinks it can force me to be one of your weak-kneed sentimentalists who let everybody do what they like——

RALPH. There are a good many who stand on their rights left, John.

BUILDER. [*Absorbed*] What! How can men stand on their rights left?

JOURNALIST. I'm afraid you had a painful experience, sir.

BUILDER. Every kind of humiliation. I spent the night in a stinking cell. I haven't eaten since breakfast yesterday. Did they think I was going to eat the muck they shoved in? And all because in a moment of anger—which I regret, I regret!—I happened to strike my daughter, who was interfering between me and my wife. The thing would be funny if it weren't so disgusting. A man's house used to be sanctuary. What is it now? With all the world poking their noses in?

He stands before the fire with his head bent, excluding as it were his interviewer and all the world.

JOURNALIST. [*Preparing to go*] Thank you very much, Mr. Builder. I'm sure I can do you justice. Would you like to see a proof?

BUILDER. [*Half conscious of him*] What?

JOURNALIST. Or will you trust me?

BUILDER. I wouldn't trust you a yard.

JOURNALIST. [*At the door*] Very well, sir; you shall have a proof, I promise. Good afternoon, and thank you.

BUILDER. Here!

But he is gone, and BUILDER *is left staring at his brother, on whose face is still that look of whimsical commiseration.*

RALPH. Take a pull, old man! Have a hot bath and go to bed.

BUILDER. They've chosen to drive me to extremes, now let them take the consequences. I don't care a kick what anybody thinks.

RALPH. [*Sadly*] Well, I won't worry you any more, now.

BUILDER. [*With a nasty laugh*] No; come again to-morrow!

RALPH. When you've had a sleep. For the sake of the family name, John, don't be hasty.

BUILDER. Shut the stable door? No, my boy, the horse has gone.

RALPH. Well, well!

With a lingering look at his brother, who has sat down sullenly at the writing-table, he goes out into the hall.

BUILDER *remains staring in front of him. The dining-room door opens, and* CAMILLE'S *head is thrust in. Seeing him, she draws back, but he catches sight of her.*

BUILDER. Here!

CAMILLE *comes doubtfully up to the writing-*

table. Her forehead is puckered as if she were thinking hard.

BUILDER. [*Looking at her, unsmiling*] So you want to be my mistress, do you?

[CAMILLE *makes a nervous gesture.*

Well, you shall. Come here.

CAMILLE. [*Not moving*] You f-frighten me.

BUILDER. I've paid a pretty price for you. But you'll make up for it; you and others.

CAMILLE. [*Starting back*] No; I don't like you to-day! No!

BUILDER. Come along! [*She is just within reach and he seizes her arm*] All my married life I've put a curb on myself for the sake of respectability. I've been a man of principle, my girl, as you saw yesterday. Well, they don't want that! [*He draws her close*] You can sit on my knee now.

CAMILLE. [*Shrinking*] No; I don't want to, to-day.

BUILDER. But you shall. They've asked for it!

CAMILLE. [*With a supple movement slipping away from him*] They? What is all that? I don't want any trouble. No, no; I am not taking any.

She moves back towards the door. BUILDER *utters a sardonic laugh.*

Oh! you are a dangerous man! No, no! Not for me! Good-bye, sare!

[*She turns swiftly and goes out.*

BUILDER *again utters his glum laugh. And then, as he sits alone staring before him, perfect silence reigns in the room. Over the window-sill behind him a* BOY'S *face is seen to rise; it hangs there a moment with a grin spreading on it.*

BOY'S VOICE. [*Sotto*] Johnny Builder!

[*As* BUILDER *turns sharply, it vanishes.*

'Oo beat 'is wife?

[BUILDER *rushes to the window.*

BOY'S VOICE. [*More distant and a little tentative*] Johnny Builder!

BUILDER. You little devil! If I catch you, I'll wring your blasted little neck!

BOY'S VOICE. [*A little distant*] 'Oo blacked the copper's eye?

BUILDER, *in an ungovernable passion, seizes a small flower-pot from the sill and flings it with all his force. The sound of a crash.*

BOY'S VOICE. [*Very distant*] Ya-a-ah! Missed!

BUILDER *stands leaning out, face injected with blood, shaking his fist.*

The CURTAIN *falls for a few seconds.*

SCENE III

Evening the same day.

BUILDER'S *study is dim and neglected-looking; the window is still open, though it has become night. A street lamp outside shines in, and the end of its rays fall on* BUILDER *asleep. He is sitting in a high chair at the fireside end of the writing-table, with his elbows on it, and his cheek resting on his hand. He is still unshaven, and his clothes unchanged. A* BOY'S *head appears above the level of the window-sill, as if beheaded and fastened there.*

BOY'S VOICE. [*In a forceful whisper*] Johnny Builder!

BUILDER *stirs uneasily. The* BOY'S *head vanishes.* BUILDER, *raising his other hand, makes a sweep before his face, as if to brush away a mosquito. He wakes. Takes in remembrance, and sits a moment staring gloomily before him. The door from the hall is opened and* TOPPING *comes in with a long envelope in his hand.*

TOPPING. [*Approaching*] From the "Comet," sir. Proof of your interview, sir; will you please revise, the messenger says; he wants to take it back at once.

BUILDER. [*Taking it*] All right. I'll ring.

TOPPING. Shall I close in, sir?

BUILDER. Not now.

[TOPPING *withdraws.*

BUILDER *turns up a standard lamp on the table, opens the envelope, and begins reading the galley slip. The signs of uneasiness and discomfort grow on him.*

BUILDER. Did I say that? Muck! Muck! [*He drops the proof, sits a moment moving his head and rubbing one hand uneasily on the surface of the table, then reaches out for the telephone receiver*] Town, 245. [*Pause*] The "Comet"? John Builder. Give me the Editor. [*Pause*] That you, Mr. Editor? John Builder speaking. That interview. I've got the proof. It won't do. Scrap the whole thing, please. I don't want to say anything. [*Pause*] Yes. I know I said it all; I can't help that. [*Pause*] No; I've changed my mind. Scrap it, please. [*Pause*] No, I will not say anything. [*Pause*] *You* can say what you dam' well please. [*Pause*] I mean it; if you put a word into my mouth, I'll sue you for defamation of character. It's undignified muck. I'm tearing it up. Good-night.

[*He replaces the receiver, and touches a bell; then, taking up the galley slip, he tears it viciously across into many pieces, and rams them into the envelope.*

[TOPPING *enters.*

Here, give this to the messenger—sharp, and tell him to run with it.

TOPPING. [*Whose hand can feel the condition of the contents, with a certain surprise*] Yes, sir.

[*He goes, with a look back from the door.*

The Mayor is here, sir. I don't know whether you would wish——

BUILDER, *rising, takes a turn up and down the room.*

BUILDER. Nor do I. Yes! I'll see him.

TOPPING *goes out, and* BUILDER *stands over by the fender, with his head a little down.*

TOPPING. [*Re-entering*] The Mayor, sir.

[*He retires up Left.*

The MAYOR *is overcoated, and carries, of all*

things, a top hat. He reaches the centre of the room before he speaks.

MAYOR. [*Embarrassed*] Well, Builder?

BUILDER. Well?

MAYOR. Come! That caution of mine was quite parliamentary. I 'ad to save face, you know.

BUILDER. And what about my face?

MAYOR. Well, you—you made it difficult for me. 'Ang it all! Put yourself into my place!

BUILDER. [*Grimly*] I'd rather put you into mine, as it was last night.

MAYOR. Yes, yes! I know; but the Bench has got a name to keep up—must stand well in the people's eyes. As it is, I sailed very near the wind. Suppose we had an ordinary person up before us for striking a woman?

BUILDER. I didn't strike a woman—I struck my daughter.

MAYOR. Well, but she's not a child, you know. And you did resist the police, if no worse. Come! You'd have been the first to maintain British justice. Shake 'ands!

BUILDER. Is that what you came for?

MAYOR. [*Taken back*] Why—yes; nobody can be more sorry than I——

BUILDER. Eye-wash! You came to beg me to resign.

MAYOR. Well, it's precious awkward, Builder. We all feel——

BUILDER. Save your powder, Mayor. I've slept

on it since I wrote you that note. Take my resignations.

MAYOR. [*In relieved embarrassment*] That's right. We must face your position.

BUILDER. [*With a touch of grim humour*] I never yet met a man who couldn't face another man's position.

MAYOR. After all, what is it?

BUILDER. Splendid isolation. No wife, no daughters, no Councillorship, no Magistracy, no future—[*With a laugh*] not even a French maid. And why? Because I tried to exercise a little wholesome family authority. That's the position you're facing, Mayor.

MAYOR. Dear, dear! You're devilish bitter, Builder. It's unfortunate, this publicity. But it'll all blow over; and you'll be back where you were. You've a *good* sound practical sense underneath your temper. [*A pause*] Come, now! [*A pause*] Well, I'll say good-night, then.

BUILDER. You shall have them in writing to-morrow.

MAYOR. [*With sincerity*] Come! Shake 'ands.

BUILDER, *after a long look, holds out his hand. The two men exchange a grip. The* MAYOR, *turning abruptly, goes out.*

BUILDER *remains motionless for a minute, then resumes his seat at the side of the writing-table, leaning his head on his hands.*

The BOY'S *head is again seen rising above the level of the window-sill, and another and another follows, till the three, as if decapitated, heads are seen in a row.*

BOYS' VOICES. [*One after another in a whispered*

crescendo] Johnny Builder! Johnny Builder! Johnny Builder!

BUILDER *rises, turns and stares at them. The* THREE HEADS *disappear, and a* BOY'S *voice cries shrilly: "Johnny Builder!"* BUILDER *moves towards the window; voices are now crying in various pitches and keys: "Johnny Builder!" "Beatey Builder!" "Beat 'is wife-er!" "Beatey Builder!"* BUILDER *stands quite motionless, staring, with the street lamp lighting up a queer, rather pitiful defiance on his face. The voices swell. There comes a sudden swish and splash of water, and broken yells of dismay.*

TOPPING'S VOICE. Scat! you young devils!

The sound of scuffling feet and a long-drawn-out and distant "Miaou!"

BUILDER *stirs, shuts the window, draws the curtains, goes to the armchair before the fireplace and sits down in it.*

TOPPING *enters with a little tray on which is a steaming jug of fluid, some biscuits and a glass. He comes stealthily up level with the chair.* BUILDER *stirs and looks up at him.*

TOPPING. Excuse me, sir, you must 'ave digested yesterday morning's breakfast by now—must live to eat, sir.

BUILDER. All right. Put it down.

TOPPING. [*Putting the tray down on the table and*

taking up BUILDER's *pipe*] I fair copped those young devils.

BUILDER. You're a good fellow.

TOPPING. [*Filling the pipe*] You'll excuse me, sir; the Missis—has come back, sir——

BUILDER *stares at him and* TOPPING *stops. He hands* BUILDER *the filled pipe and a box of matches.*

BUILDER. [*With a shiver*] Light the fire, Topping. I'm chilly.

While TOPPING *lights the fire* BUILDER *puts the pipe in his mouth and applies a match to it.* TOPPING, *having lighted the fire, turns to go, gets as far as half way, then comes back level with the table and regards the silent brooding figure in the chair.*

BUILDER. [*Suddenly*] Give me that paper on the table. No; the other one—the Will.

TOPPING *takes up the Will and gives it to him.*

TOPPING. [*With much hesitation*] Excuse me, sir. It's pluck that get's 'em 'ome, sir—begging your pardon.

BUILDER *has resumed his attitude and does not answer.*

[*In a voice just touched with feeling*] Good-night, sir.

BUILDER. [*Without turning his head*] Good-night.

[TOPPING *has gone.*

BUILDER *sits drawing at his pipe between the firelight and the light from the standard lamp. He takes the pipe out of his mouth and a quiver passes over his face. With a half angry gesture he rubs the back of his hand across his eyes.*

BUILDER. [*To himself*] Pluck! Pluck! [*His lips quiver again. He presses them hard together, puts his pipe back into his mouth, and, taking the Will, thrusts it into the newly-lighted fire and holds it there with a poker*].

While he is doing this the door from the hall is opened quietly, and MRS. BUILDER *enters without his hearing her. She has a work-bag in her hand. She moves slowly to the table, and stands looking at him. Then going up to the curtains she mechanically adjusts them, and still keeping her eyes on* BUILDER, *comes down to the table and pours out his usual glass of whisky toddy.* BUILDER, *who has become conscious of her presence, turns in his chair as she hands it to him. He sits a moment motionless, then takes it from her, and squeezes her hand.* MRS. BUILDER *goes silently to her usual chair below the fire, and taking out some knitting begins to knit.* BUILDER *makes an effort to speak, does not succeed, and sits drawing at his pipe.*

The CURTAIN *falls.*

LOYALTIES

A DRAMA IN THREE ACTS

PERSONS OF THE PLAY

In the Order of Appearance

Charles Winsor . .	Owner of Meldon Court, near Newmarket
Lady Adela . . .	His Wife
Ferdinand De Levis .	Young, rich, and new
Treisure . . .	Winsor's Butler
General Canynge .	A Racing Oracle
Margaret Orme . .	A Society Girl
Captain Ronald Dancy, D.S.O. . . .	Retired
Mabel	His Wife
Inspector Dede . .	Of the County Constabulary
Robert . . .	Winsor's Footman
A Constable . .	Attendant on Dede
Augustus Borring .	A Clubman
Lord St Erth . .	A Peer of the Realm
A Footman . . .	Of the Club
Major Colford . .	A Brother Officer of Dancy's
Edward Graviter .	A Solicitor
A Young Clerk . .	Of Twisden & Graviter's
Gilman . . .	A Large Grocer
Jacob Twisden . .	Senior Partner of Twisden & Graviter's
Ricardos . . .	An Italian, in Wine

ACT I.

SCENE I. CHARLES WINSOR'S *Dressing-room at Meldon Court, near Newmarket, of a night in early October.*

SCENE II. DE LEVIS'S *Bedroom at Meldon Court, a few minutes later.*

ACT II.

SCENE I. *The Card Room of a London Club between four and five in the afternoon, three weeks later.*

SCENE II. *The Sitting-room of the* DANCYS' *Flat, the following morning.*

ACT III.

SCENE I. *Old* MR JACOB TWISDEN'S *Room at Twisden &* GRAVITER'S *in Lincoln's Inn Fields, at four in the afternoon, three months later.*

SCENE II. *The same, next morning at half-past ten.*

SCENE III. *The Sitting-room of the* DANCYS' *Flat, an hour later.*

ACT I

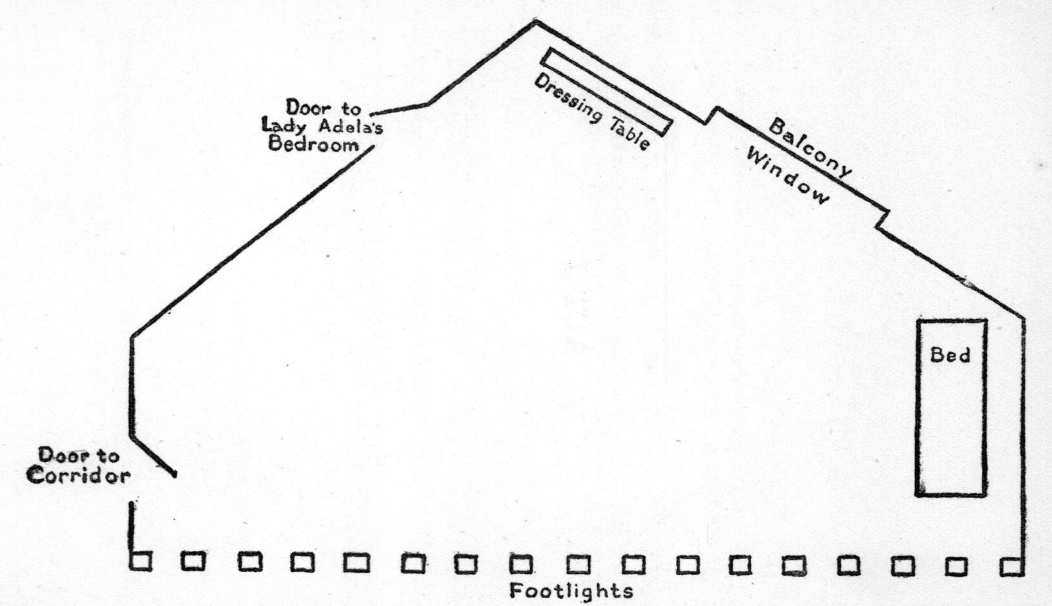

Door to
Lady Adela's
Bedroom
Dressing Table
Balcony
Window
Bed
Door to
Corridor
Footlights

ACT I

SCENE I

The dressing-room of CHARLES WINSOR, *owner of Meldon Court, near Newmarket; about eleven-thirty at night. The room has pale grey walls, unadorned; the curtains are drawn over a window Back Left Centre. A bed lies along the wall, Left. An open door, Right Back, leads into* LADY ADELA'S *bedroom; a door, Right Forward, into a long corridor, on to which abut rooms in a row, the whole length of the house's left wing.* WINSOR'S *dressing-table, with a light over it, is Stage Right of the curtained window. Pyjamas are laid out on the bed, which is turned back. Slippers are handy, and all the usual gear of a well-appointed bed-dressing-room.* CHARLES WINSOR, *a tall, fair, good-looking man about thirty-eight, is taking off a smoking jacket.*

WINSOR. Hallo! Adela!

V. OF LADY A. [*From her bedroom*] Hallo!

WINSOR. In bed?

V. OF LADY A. No.

She appears in the doorway in under-garment and a wrapper. She, too, is fair, about thirty-five, rather delicious, and suggestive of porcelain.

WINSOR. Win at Bridge?

LADY A. No fear.

WINSOR. Who did?

LADY A. Lord St Erth and Ferdy De Levis.

WINSOR. That young man has too much luck—the young bounder won two races to-day; and he's as rich as Crœsus.

LADY A. Oh! Charlie, he did look so exactly as if he'd sold me a carpet when I was paying him.

WINSOR. [*Changing into slippers*] His father did sell carpets, wholesale, in the City.

LADY A. Really? And you say I haven't intuition! [*With a finger on her lips*] Morison's in there.

WINSOR. [*Motioning towards the door, which she shuts*] Ronny Dancy took a tenner off him, anyway, before dinner.

LADY A. No! How?

WINSOR. Standing jump on to a bookcase four feet high. De Levis had to pay up, and sneered at him for making money by parlour tricks. That young Jew gets himself disliked.

LADY A. Aren't you rather prejudiced?

WINSOR. Not a bit. I like Jews. That's not against him—rather the contrary these days. But he pushes himself. The General tells me he's deathly keen to get into the Jockey Club. [*Taking off his tie*] It's amusing to see him trying to get round old St Erth.

LADY A. If Lord St Erth and General Canynge backed him he'd get in if he *did* sell carpets!

WINSOR. He's got some pretty good horses. [*Taking off his waistcoat*] Ronny Dancy's on his bones again, I'm afraid. He had a bad day. When a chap takes to doing parlour stunts for a bet—it's a sure sign. What made him chuck the Army?

LADY A. He says it's too dull, now there's no fighting.

WINSOR. Well, he can't exist on backing losers.

LADY A. Isn't it just like him to get married now? He really is the most reckless person.

WINSOR. Yes. He's a queer chap. I've always liked him, but I've never quite made him out. What do you think of his wife?

LADY A. Nice child; awfully gone on him.

WINSOR. Is *he?*

LADY A. Quite indecently—both of them. [*Nodding towards the wall, Left*] They're next door.

WINSOR. Who's beyond them?

LADY A. De Levis; and Margaret Orme at the end. Charlie, do you realise that the bathroom out there has to wash those four?

WINSOR. I know.

LADY A. Your grandfather was crazy when he built this wing; six rooms in a row with balconies like an hotel, and only one bath—if we hadn't put ours in.

WINSOR. [*Looking at his watch*] Half-past eleven. [*Yawns*] Newmarket always makes me sleepy. You're keeping Morison up.

LADY ADELA *goes to the door, blowing a kiss.* CHARLES *goes up to his dressing-table and begins to brush his hair, sprinkling on essence. There is a knock on the corridor door.*

Come in.

DE LEVIS *enters, clad in pyjamas and flowered dressing-gown. He is a dark, good-looking, rather Eastern young man. His face is long and disturbed.*

Hallo! De Levis! Anything I can do for you?

DE LEVIS. [*In a voice whose faint exoticism is broken by a vexed excitement*] I say, I'm awfully sorry, Winsor, but I thought I'd better tell you at once. I've just had—er—rather a lot of money stolen.

WINSOR. What! [*There is something of outrage in his tone and glance, as who should say: "In my house?"*] How do you mean *stolen?*

DE LEVIS. I put it under my pillow and went to have a bath; when I came back it was gone.

WINSOR. Good Lord! How much?

DE LEVIS. Nearly a thousand—nine hundred and seventy, I think.

WINSOR. Phew! [*Again the faint tone of outrage, that a man should have so much money about him*].

DE LEVIS. I sold my Rosemary filly to-day on the course to Kentman the bookie, and he paid me in notes.

WINSOR. What? That weed Dancy gave you in the Spring?

DE LEVIS. Yes. But I tried her pretty high the

other day; and she's in the Cambridgeshire. I was only out of my room a quarter of an hour, and I locked my door.

WINSOR. [*Again outraged*] You *locked*——

DE LEVIS. [*Not seeing the fine shade*] Yes, and had the key here. [*He taps his pocket*] Look here! [*He holds out a pocket-book*] It's been stuffed with my shaving papers.

WINSOR. [*Between feeling that such things don't happen, and a sense that he will have to clear it up*] This is damned awkward, De Levis.

DE LEVIS. [*With steel in his voice*] Yes. I should like it back.

WINSOR. Have you got the numbers of the notes?

DE LEVIS. No.

WINSOR. What were they?

DE LEVIS. One hundred, three fifties, and the rest tens and fives.

WINSOR. What d'you want me to do?

DE LEVIS. Unless there's anybody you think——

WINSOR. [*Eyeing him*] Is it likely?

DE LEVIS. Then I think the police ought to see my room. It's a lot of money.

WINSOR. Good Lord! We're not in Town; there'll be nobody nearer than Newmarket at this time of night—four miles.

The door from the bedroom is suddenly opened and LADY ADELA *appears. She has on a lace cap over her finished hair, and the wrapper.*

LADY A. [*Closing the door*] What is it? Are you ill, Mr De Levis?

WINSOR. Worse; he's had a lot of money stolen. Nearly a thousand pounds.

LADY A. Gracious! Where?

DE LEVIS. From under my pillow, Lady Adela—my door was locked—I was in the bathroom.

LADY A. But how fearfully thrilling!

WINSOR. Thrilling! What's to be done? He wants it back.

LADY A. Of course! [*With sudden realisation*] Oh! But—— Oh! it's quite too unpleasant!

WINSOR. Yes! What am I to do? Fetch the servants out of their rooms? Search the grounds? It'll make the devil of a scandal.

DE LEVIS. Who's next to me?

LADY A. [*Coldly*] Oh! Mr De Levis!

WINSOR. Next to you? The Dancys on this side, and Miss Orme on the other. What's that to do with it?

DE LEVIS. They may have heard something.

WINSOR. Let's get them. But Dancy was downstairs when I came up. Get Morison, Adela! No, Look here! When *was* this exactly? Let's have as many alibis as we can.

DE LEVIS. Within the last twenty minutes, certainly.

WINSOR. How long has Morison been up with you?

LADY A. I came up at eleven, and rang for her at once.

WINSOR. [*Looking at his watch*] Half an hour. Then she's all right. Send her for Margaret and the Dancys — there's nobody else in this wing. No; send her to bed. We don't want gossip. D'you mind going yourself, Adela?

LADY A. Consult General Canynge, Charlie.

WINSOR. Right. Could you get him too? D'you really want the police, De Levis?

DE LEVIS. [*Stung by the faint contempt in his tone of voice*] Yes, I do.

WINSOR. Then, look here, dear! Slip into my study and telephone to the police at Newmarket. There'll be somebody there; they're sure to have drunks. I'll have Treisure up, and speak to him. [*He rings the bell*].

LADY ADELA *goes out into her room and closes the door.*

WINSOR. Look here, De Levis! This isn't an hotel. It's the sort of thing that doesn't happen in a decent house. Are you sure you're not mistaken, and didn't have them stolen on the course?

DE LEVIS. Absolutely. I counted them just before putting them under my pillow; then I locked the door and had the key here. There's only one door, you know.

WINSOR. How was your window?

DE LEVIS. Open.

WINSOR. [*Drawing back the curtains of his own window*] You've got a balcony like this. Any sign of a ladder or anything?

DE LEVIS. No.

WINSOR. It must have been done from the window, unless someone had a skeleton key. Who knew you'd got that money? Where did Kentman pay you?

DE LEVIS. Just round the corner in the further paddock.

WINSOR. Anybody about?

DE LEVIS. Oh, yes!

WINSOR. Suspicious?

DE LEVIS. I didn't notice anything.

WINSOR. You must have been marked down and followed here.

DE LEVIS. How would they know my room?

WINSOR. Might have got it somehow. [*A knock from the corridor*] Come in.

TREISURE, *the Butler, appears, a silent, grave man of almost supernatural conformity.* DE LEVIS *gives him a quick, hard look, noted and resented by* WINSOR.

TREISURE. [*To* WINSOR] Yes, sir?

WINSOR. Who valets Mr De Levis?

TREISURE. Robert, sir.

WINSOR. When was he up last?

TREISURE. In the ordinary course of things, about ten o'clock, sir.

WINSOR. When did he go to bed?

TREISURE. I dismissed at eleven.

WINSOR. But did he go?

TREISURE. To the best of my knowledge. Is there anything *I* can do, sir?

WINSOR. [*Disregarding a sign from* DE LEVIS]

Look here, Treisure, Mr De Levis has had a large sum of money taken from his bedroom within the last half hour.

TREISURE. Indeed, sir!

WINSOR. Robert's quite all right, isn't he?

TREISURE. He is, sir.

DE LEVIS. How do you know?

TREISURE'S *eyes rest on* DE LEVIS.

TREISURE. I am a pretty good judge of character, sir, if you'll excuse me.

WINSOR. Look here, De Levis, eighty or ninety notes must have been pretty bulky. You didn't have them on you at dinner?

DE LEVIS. No.

WINSOR. Where did you put them?

DE LEVIS. In a boot, and the boot in my suit-case, and locked it.

TREISURE *smiles faintly.*

WINSOR. [*Again slightly outraged by such precautions in his house*] And you found it locked—and took them from there to put under your pillow?

DE LEVIS. Yes.

WINSOR. Run your mind over things, Treisure—has any stranger been about?

TREISURE. No, sir.

WINSOR. This seems to have happened between 11.15 and 11.30. Is that right? [DE LEVIS *nods*] Any noise—anything outside—anything suspicious anywhere?

TREISURE. [*Running his mind—very still*] No, sir.

WINSOR. What time did you shut up?

TREISURE. I should say about eleven-fifteen, sir. As soon as Major Colford and Captain Dancy had finished billiards. What was Mr De Levis doing out of his room, if I may ask, sir?

WINSOR. Having a bath; with his room locked and the key in his pocket.

TREISURE. Thank you, sir.

DE LEVIS. [*Conscious of indefinable suspicion*] Damn it! What do you mean? I *was*.

TREISURE. I beg your pardon, sir.

WINSOR. [*Concealing a smile*] Look here, Treisure, it's infernally awkward for everybody.

TREISURE. It is, sir.

WINSOR. What do you suggest?

TREISURE. The proper thing, sir, I suppose, would be a cordon and a complete search—in our interests.

WINSOR. I entirely refuse to suspect anybody.

TREISURE. But if Mr De Levis feels otherwise, sir?

DE LEVIS. [*Stammering*] I? All I know is—the money was there, and it's gone.

WINSOR. [*Compunctious*] Quite! It's pretty sickening for you. But so it is for anybody else. However, we must do our best to get it back for you.

A knock on the door.

WINSOR. Hallo!

TREISURE *opens the door, and* GENERAL CANYNGE *enters.*

Oh! It's you, General. Come in. Adela's told you?

GENERAL CANYNGE *nods. He is a slim man*

of about sixty, very well preserved, intensely neat and self-contained, and still in evening dress. His eyelids droop slightly, but his eyes are keen and his expression astute.

WINSOR. Well, General, what's the first move?

CANYNGE. [*Lifting his eyebrows*] Mr De Levis presses the matter?

DE LEVIS. [*Flicked again*] Unless you think it's too plebeian of me, General Canynge—a thousand pounds.

CANYNGE. [*Drily*] Just so! Then we must wait for the police, Winsor. Lady Adela has got through to them. What height are these rooms from the ground, Treisure?

TREISURE. Twenty-three feet from the terrace, sir.

CANYNGE. Any ladders near?

TREISURE. One in the stables, sir, very heavy. No others within three hundred yards.

CANYNGE. Just slip down, and see whether that's been moved.

TREISURE. Very good, General. [*He goes out.*]

DE LEVIS. [*Uneasily*] Of course, he—I suppose you——

WINSOR. We do.

CANYNGE. You had better leave this in our hands, De Levis.

DE LEVIS. Certainly; only, the way he——

WINSOR. [*Curtly*] Treisure has been here since he was a boy. I should as soon suspect myself.

DE LEVIS. [*Looking from one to the other—with*

sudden anger] You seem to think——! What was I to do? Take it lying down and let whoever it is get clear off? I suppose it's natural to want my money back?

CANYNGE *looks at his nails;* WINSOR *out of the window.*

WINSOR. [*Turning*] Of course, De Levis!

DE LEVIS. [*Sullenly*] Well, I'll go to my room. When the police come, perhaps you'll let me know.

He goes out.

WINSOR. Phew! Did you ever see such a dressing-gown?

The door is opened. LADY ADELA *and* MARGARET ORME *come in. The latter is a vivid young lady of about twenty-five in a vivid wrapper; she is smoking a cigarette.*

LADY A. I've told the Dancys—she was in bed. And I got through to Newmarket, Charles, and Inspector Dede is coming like the wind on a motor cycle.

MARGARET. Did he say "like the wind," Adela? He must have imagination. Isn't this gorgeous? Poor little Ferdy!

WINSOR. [*Vexed*] You might take it seriously, Margaret; it's pretty beastly for us all. What time did *you* come up?

MARGARET. I came up with Adela. Am I suspected, Charles? How thrilling!

WINSOR. Did you hear anything?

MARGARET. Only little Ferdy splashing.

WINSOR. And saw nothing?

MARGARET. Not even that, alas!

LADY A. [*With a finger held up*] *Leste! Un peu leste!* Oh! Here are the Dancys. Come in, you two!

MABEL *and* RONALD DANCY *enter. She is a pretty young woman with bobbed hair, fortunately, for she has just got out of bed, and is in her nightgown and a wrapper.* DANCY *is in his smoking jacket. He has a pale, determined face with high cheekbones, small, deep-set dark eyes, reddish crisp hair, and looks like a horseman.*

WINSOR. Awfully sorry to disturb you, Mrs Dancy; but I suppose you and Ronny haven't heard anything. De Levis's room is just beyond Ronny's dressing-room, you know.

MABEL. I've been asleep nearly half an hour, and Ronny's only just come up.

CANYNGE. Did you happen to look out of your window, Mrs Dancy?

MABEL. Yes. I stood there quite five minutes.

CANYNGE. When?

MABEL. Just about eleven, I should think. It was raining hard then.

CANYNGE. Yes, it's just stopped. You saw nothing?

MABEL. No.

DANCY. What time does he say the money was taken?

WINSOR. Between the quarter and half past. He'd locked his door and had the key with him.

MARGARET. How quaint! Just like an hotel. Does he put his boots out?

LADY A. Don't be so naughty, Meg.

CANYNGE. When exactly did *you* come up, Dancy?

DANCY. About ten minutes ago. I'd only just got into my dressing-room before Lady Adela came. I've been writing letters in the hall since Colford and I finished billiards.

CANYNGE. You weren't up for anything in between?

DANCY. No.

MARGARET. The mystery of the grey room.

DANCY. Oughtn't the grounds to be searched for footmarks?

CANYNGE. That's for the police.

DANCY. The deuce! Are they coming?

CANYNGE. Directly. [*A knock*] Yes?

TREISURE *enters*.

Well?

TREISURE. The ladder has not been moved, General. There isn't a sign.

WINSOR. All right. Get Robert up, but don't say anything to him. By the way, we're expecting the police.

TREISURE. I trust they will not find a mare's nest, sir, if I may say so.

He goes.

WINSOR. De Levis has got wrong with Treisure. [*Suddenly*] But, I say, what would any of us have done if *we'd* been in his shoes?

MARGARET. A thousand pounds? I can't even conceive having it.

DANCY. We probably shouldn't have found it out.

LADY A. No—but if we had.

DANCY. Come to you—as he did.

WINSOR. Yes; but there's a way of doing things.

CANYNGE. We shouldn't have wanted the police.

MARGARET. No. That's it. The hotel touch.

LADY A. Poor young man; I think we're rather hard on him.

WINSOR. He sold that weed you gave him, Dancy, to Kentman, the bookie, and these were the proceeds.

DANCY. Oh!

WINSOR. He'd tried her high, he said.

DANCY. [*Grimly*] He would.

MABEL. Oh! Ronny, what bad luck!

WINSOR. He must have been followed here. [*At the window*] After rain like that, there ought to be footmarks.

The splutter of a motor cycle is heard.

MARGARET. Here's the wind!

WINSOR. What's the move now, General?

CANYNGE. You and I had better see the Inspector in De Levis's room, Winsor. [*To the others*] If you'll all be handy, in case he wants to put questions for himself.

MARGARET. I hope he'll want me; it's just too thrilling.

DANCY. I hope he won't want me; I'm dog-tired. Come on, Mabel. [*He puts his arm in his wife's*].

CANYNGE. Just a minute, Charles.

He draws close to WINSOR *as the others are departing to their rooms.*

WINSOR. Yes, General?

CANYNGE. We must be careful with this Inspector fellow. If he pitches hastily on somebody in the house it'll be very disagreeable.

WINSOR. By Jove! It *will*.

CANYNGE. We don't want to rouse any ridiculous suspicion.

WINSOR. Quite. [*A knock*] Come in!

TREISURE *enters.*

TREISURE. Inspector Dede, sir.

WINSOR. Show him in.

TREISURE. Robert is in readiness, sir; but I could swear he knows nothing about it.

WINSOR. All right.

TREISURE *reopens the door, and says: "Come in, please." The* INSPECTOR *enters, blue, formal, moustachioed, with a peaked cap in his hand.*

WINSOR. Good-evening, Inspector. Sorry to have brought you out at this time of night.

INSPECTOR. Good evenin', sir. Mr Winsor? You're the owner here, I think?

WINSOR. Yes. General Canynge.

INSPECTOR. Good evenin', General. I understand, a large sum of money?

WINSOR. Yes. Shall we go straight to the room

it was taken from? One of my guests, Mr De Levis. It's the third room on the left.

CANYNGE. We've not been in there yet, Inspector; in fact, we've done nothing, except to find out that the stable ladder has not been moved. We haven't even searched the grounds.

INSPECTOR. Right, sir; I've brought a man with me.

They go out.

CURTAIN. *Interval of a Minute.*

De Levis. [*Pointing*] Where it is now—under the dressing-table.

He comes forward to the front of the chair, opens the pocket-book, goes through the pretence of counting his shaving papers, closes the pocket-book, takes it to the head of the bed and slips it under the pillow. Makes the motion of taking up his pyjamas, crosses below the Inspector *to the wash-stand, takes up a bath sponge, crosses to the door, takes out the key, opens the door.*

Inspector. [*Writing*]. We now have the room as it was when the theft was committed. Reconstruct accordin' to 'uman nature, gentlemen—assumin' the thief to be in the room, what would he try first?—the clothes, the dressin'-table, the suit case, the chest of drawers, and last the bed.

He moves accordingly, examining the glass on the dressing-table, the surface of the suit cases, and the handles of the drawers, with a spy-glass, for finger-marks.

Canynge. [*Sotto voce to* Winsor] The order would have been just the other way.

The Inspector *goes on hands and knees and examines the carpet between the window and the bed.*

De Levis. Can I come in again?

Inspector. [*Standing up*] Did you open the window, sir, or was it open when you first came in?

De Levis. I opened it.

Inspector. Drawin' the curtains back first?

DE LEVIS. Yes.

INSPECTOR. [*Sharply*] Are you sure there was nobody in the room already?

DE LEVIS. [*Taken aback*] I don't know. I never thought. I didn't look under the bed, if you mean that.

INSPECTOR. [*Jotting*] Did not look under bed. Did you look under it after the theft?

DE LEVIS. No. I didn't.

INSPECTOR. Ah! Now, what *did* you do after you came back from your bath? Just give us that precisely.

DE LEVIS. Locked the door and left the key in. Put back my sponge, and took off my dressing-gown and put it there. [*He points to the footrails of the bed*] Then I drew the curtains, again.

INSPECTOR. Shutting the window?

DE LEVIS. No. I got into bed, felt for my watch to see the time. My hand struck the pocket-book, and somehow it felt thinner. I took it out, looked into it, and found the notes gone, and these shaving papers instead.

INSPECTOR. Let me have a look at those, sir. [*He applies the spy-glasses*] And then?

DE LEVIS. I think I just sat on the bed.

INSPECTOR. Thinkin' and cursin' a bit, I suppose. Ye-es?

DE LEVIS. Then I put on my dressing-gown and went straight to Mr Winsor.

INSPECTOR. Not lockin' the door?

DE LEVIS. No.

INSPECTOR. Exactly. [*With a certain finality*] Now, sir, what time did you come up?

DE LEVIS. About eleven.

INSPECTOR. Precise, if you can give it me.

DE LEVIS. Well, I *know* it was eleven-fifteen when I put my watch under my pillow, before I went to the bath, and I suppose I'd been about a quarter of an hour undressing. I should say after eleven, if anything.

INSPECTOR. Just undressin'? Didn't look over your bettin' book?

DE LEVIS. No.

INSPECTOR. No prayers or anything?

DE LEVIS. No.

INSPECTOR. Pretty slippy with your undressin' as a rule?

DE LEVIS. Yes. Say five past eleven.

INSPECTOR. Mr Winsor, what time did the gentleman come to you?

WINSOR. Half-past eleven.

INSPECTOR. How do you fix that, sir?

WINSOR. I'd just looked at the time, and told my wife to send her maid off.

INSPECTOR. Then we've got it fixed between 11.15 and 11.30. [*Jots*] Now, sir, before we go further I'd like to see your butler and the footman that valets this gentleman.

WINSOR. [*With distaste*] Very well, Inspector; only—my butler has been with us from a boy.

INSPECTOR. Quite so. This is just clearing the ground, sir.

WINSOR. General, d'you mind touching that bell?

CANYNGE rings a bell by the bed.

INSPECTOR. Well, gentlemen, there are four possibilities. Either the thief was here all the time, waiting under the bed, and slipped out after this gentleman had gone to Mr Winsor. Or he came in with a key that fits the lock; and I'll want to see all the keys in the house. Or he came in with a skeleton key and out by the window, probably droppin' from the balcony. Or he came in by the window with a rope or ladder and out the same way. [*Pointing*] There's a footmark here from a big boot which has been out of doors since it rained.

CANYNGE. Inspector—you er—walked up to the window when you first came into the room.

INSPECTOR. [*Stiffly*] I had not overlooked that, General.

CANYNGE. Of course.

A knock on the door relieves a certain tension.

WINSOR. Come in.

The footman ROBERT, *a fresh-faced young man, enters, followed by* TREISURE.

INSPECTOR. You valet Mr—Mr De Levis, I think?

ROBERT. Yes, sir.

INSPECTOR. At what time did you take his clothes and boots?

ROBERT. Ten o'clock, sir.

INSPECTOR. [*With a pounce*] Did you happen to look under his bed?

ROBERT. No, sir.

INSPECTOR. Did you come up again, to bring the clothes back?

ROBERT. No, sir; they're still downstairs.

INSPECTOR. Did you come up again for anything?

ROBERT. No, sir.

INSPECTOR. What time did you go to bed?

ROBERT. Just after eleven, sir.

INSPECTOR. [*Scrutinising him*] Now, be careful. Did you go to bed at all?

ROBERT. No, sir.

INSPECTOR. Then why did you say you did? There's been a theft here, and anything you say may be used against you.

ROBERT. Yes, sir. I meant, I went to my room.

INSPECTOR. Where is your room?

ROBERT. On the ground floor, at the other end of the right wing, sir.

WINSOR. It's the extreme end of the house from this, Inspector. He's with the other two footmen.

INSPECTOR. Were you there alone?

ROBERT. No, sir. Thomas and Frederick was there too.

TREISURE. That's right; I've seen them.

INSPECTOR. [*Holding up his hand for silence*] Were you out of the room again after you went in?

ROBERT. No, sir.

INSPECTOR. What were you doing, if you didn't go to bed?

ROBERT. [*To* WINSOR] Beggin' your pardon, sir, we were playin' Bridge.

INSPECTOR. Very good. You can go. I'll see *them* later on.

ROBERT. Yes, sir. They'll say the same as me.

He goes out, leaving a smile on the face of all except the INSPECTOR *and* DE LEVIS.

INSPECTOR. [*Sharply*] Call him back.

TREISURE calls "*Robert,*" *and the* FOOTMAN *re-enters.*

ROBERT. Yes, sir?

INSPECTOR. Did you notice anything particular about Mr De Levis's clothes?

ROBERT. Only that they were very good, sir.

INSPECTOR. I mean—anything peculiar?

ROBERT. [*After reflection*] Yes, sir.

INSPECTOR. Well?

ROBERT. A pair of his boots this evenin' was reduced to one, sir.

INSPECTOR. What did you make of that?

ROBERT. I thought he might have thrown the other at a cat or something.

INSPECTOR. Did you look for it?

ROBERT. No, sir; I meant to draw his attention to it in the morning.

INSPECTOR. Very good.

ROBERT. Yes, sir. [*He goes again.*]

INSPECTOR. [*Looking at* DE LEVIS] Well, sir, there's *your* story corroborated.

DE LEVIS. [*Stiffly*] I don't know why it should need corroboration, Inspector.

INSPECTOR. In my experience, you can never have too much of that. [*To* WINSOR] I understand sir. [*He makes another entry in his note-book*] Good-night, then, gentlemen!

CANYNGE. Good-night!

WINSOR. [*With relief*] I'll come with you, Inspector.

He escorts him to the door, and they go out.

DE LEVIS. [*Suddenly*] General, I know who took them.

CANYNGE. The deuce you do! Are you following the Inspector's theory?

DE LEVIS. [*Contemptuously*] That ass! [*Pulling the shaving papers out of the case*] No! The man who put those there was clever and cool enough to wrench that creeper off the balcony, as a blind. Come and look here, General. [*He goes to the window; the* GENERAL *follows.* DE LEVIS *points stage Right*] See the rail of my balcony, and the rail of the next? *He holds up the cord of his dressing-gown, stretching his arms out*] I've measured it with this. Just over seven feet, that's all! If a man can take a standing jump on to a narrow bookcase four feet high and balance there, he'd make nothing of that. And, look here! [*He goes out on the balcony and returns with a bit of broken creeper in his hand, and holds it out into the light*] Someone's stood on that—the stalk's crushed—the inner corner too, where he'd naturally stand when he took his jump back.

CANYNGE. [*After examining it—stiffly*] That other balcony is young Dancy's, Mr De Levis; a soldier and a gentleman. This is an extraordinary insinuation.

De Levis. Accusation.

Canynge. What!

De Levis. I have intuitions, General; it's in my blood. I see the whole thing. Dancy came up, watched me into the bathroom, tried my door, slipped back into his dressing-room, saw my window was open, took that jump, sneaked the notes, filled the case up with these, wrenched the creeper there [*He points stage Left*] for a blind, jumped back, and slipped downstairs again. It didn't take him four minutes altogether.

Canynge. [*Very gravely*] This is outrageous, De Levis. Dancy says he was downstairs all the time. You must either withdraw unreservedly, or I must confront you with him.

De Levis. If he'll return the notes and apologise, I'll do nothing—except cut him in future. He gave me that filly, you know, as a hopeless weed, and he's been pretty sick ever since, that he was such a flat as not to see how good she was. Besides, he's hard up, I know.

Canynge. [*After a vexed turn up and down the room*] It's mad, sir, to jump to conclusions like this.

De Levis. Not so mad as the conclusion Dancy jumped to when he lighted on my balcony.

Canynge. Nobody could have taken this money who did not know you had it.

De Levis. How do you know that he didn't?

Canynge. Do you know that he did?

De Levis. I haven't the least doubt of it.

CANYNGE. With an eye to possibilities, I venture to think—the principle guides a good many transactions.

DE LEVIS. [*As if flicked on a raw spot*] In my race, do you mean?

CANYNGE. [*Coldly*] I said nothing of the sort.

DE LEVIS. No; you don't *say* these things, any of you.

CANYNGE. Nor did I think it.

DE LEVIS. Dancy does.

WINSOR. Really, De Levis, if this is the way you repay hospitality——

DE LEVIS. Hospitality that skins my feelings and costs me a thousand pounds!

CANYNGE. Go and get Dancy, Winsor; but don't say anything to him.

WINSOR *goes out.*

CANYNGE. Perhaps you will kindly control yourself, and leave this to me.

DE LEVIS *turns to the window and lights a cigarette.* WINSOR *comes back, followed by* DANCY.

CANYNGE. For Winsor's sake, Dancy, we don't want any scandal or fuss about this affair. We've tried to make the police understand that. To my mind the whole thing turns on our finding who knew that De Levis had this money. It's about that we want to consult you.

WINSOR. Kentman paid De Levis round the corner in the further paddock, he says.

DE LEVIS *turns round from the window, so*

that he and DANCY *are staring at each other.*

CANYNGE. Did you hear anything that throws light, Dancy? As it was your filly originally, we thought perhaps you might.

DANCY. I? No.

CANYNGE. Didn't hear of the sale on the course at all?

DANCY. No.

CANYNGE. Then you can't suggest anyone who could have known? Nothing else was taken, you see.

DANCY. De Levis is known to be rolling, as I am known to be stony.

CANYNGE. There are a good many people still rolling, besides Mr De Levis, but not many people with so large a sum in their pocket-books.

DANCY. He won two races.

DE LEVIS. Do you suggest that I bet in ready money?

DANCY. I don't know how you bet, and I don't care.

CANYNGE. You can't help us, then?

DANCY. No, I can't. Anything else? [*He looks fixedly at* DE LEVIS].

CANYNGE. [*Putting his hand on* DANCY'S *arm*] Nothing else, thank you, Dancy.

DANCY *goes.* CANYNGE *puts his hand up to his face. A moment's silence.*

WINSOR. You see, De Levis? He didn't even know you'd got the money.

De Levis. Very conclusive.

Winsor. Well! You *are*——!

There is a knock on the door, and the Inspector *enters.*

Inspector. I'm just going, gentlemen. The grounds, I'm sorry to say, have yielded nothing. It's a bit of a puzzle.

Canynge. You've searched thoroughly?

Inspector. We have, General. I can pick up nothing near the terrace.

Winsor. [*After a look at* De Levis, *whose face expresses too much*] H'm! You'll take it up from the other end, then, Inspector?

Inspector. Well, we'll see what we can do with the bookmakers about the numbers, sir. Before I go, gentlemen — you've had time to think it over—there's no one you suspect in the house, I suppose?

De Levis's *face is alive and uncertain.* Canynge *is staring at him very fixedly.*

Winsor. [*Emphatically*] No.

De Levis *turns and goes out on to the balcony.*

Inspector. If you're coming in to the racing to-morrow, sir, you might give us a call. I'll have seen Kentman by then.

Winsor. Right you are, Inspector. Good-night, and many thanks.

Inspector. You're welcome, sir. [*He goes out.*]

Winsor. Gosh! I thought that chap [*With a nod towards the balcony*] was going to——! Look here, General, we *must* stop his tongue. Imagine it going the rounds. They may never find the real thief, you know. It's the very devil for Dancy.

CANYNGE. Winsor! Dancy's sleeve was damp.

WINSOR. How d'you mean?

CANYNGE. Quite damp. It's been raining.

The two look at each other.

WINSOR. I—I don't follow—— [*His voice is hesitative and lower, showing that he does*].

CANYNGE. It was coming down hard; a minute out in it would have been enough—— [*He motions with his chin towards the balcony*].

WINSOR. [*Hastily*] He must have been out on his balcony since.

CANYNGE. It stopped before I came up, half an hour ago.

WINSOR. He's been leaning on the wet stone, then.

CANYNGE. With the outside of the *upper* part of the arm?

WINSOR. Against the wall, perhaps. There may be a dozen explanations. [*Very low and with great concentration*] I entirely and absolutely refuse to believe anything of the sort against Ronald Dancy—in my house. Dash it, General, we must do as we'd be done by. It hits us all—it hits us all. The thing's intolerable.

CANYNGE. I agree. Intolerable. [*Raising his voice*] Mr De Levis!

DE LEVIS *returns into view, in the centre of the open window.*

CANYNGE. [*With cold decision*] Young Dancy was an officer and is a gentleman; this insinuation is pure supposition, and you must not make it. Do you understand me?

De Levis. My tongue is still mine, General, if my money isn't!

Canynge. [*Unmoved*] Must not. You're a member of three Clubs, you want to be member of a fourth. No one who makes such an insinuation against a fellow-guest in a country house, except on absolute proof, can do so without complete ostracism. Have we your word to say nothing?

De Levis. Social blackmail? H'm!

Canynge. Not at all—simple warning. If you consider it necessary in your interests to start this scandal—no matter how, we shall consider it necessary in ours to dissociate ourselves completely from one who so recklessly disregards the unwritten code.

De Levis. Do you think your code applies to me? Do you, General?

Canynge. To anyone who aspires to be a gentleman, sir.

De Levis. Ah! But you haven't known *me* since I was a boy.

Canynge. Make up your mind.

A pause.

De Levis. I'm not a fool, General. I know perfectly well that you can get me outed.

Canynge. [*Icily*] Well?

De Levis [*Sullenly*] I'll say nothing about it, unless I get more proof.

Canynge. Good! We have implicit faith in Dancy.

There is a moment's encounter of eyes; the GENERAL'S *steady, shrewd, impassive;* WINSOR'S *angry and defiant;* DE LEVIS'S *mocking, a little triumphant, malicious. Then* CANYNGE *and* WINSOR *go to the door, and pass out.*

DE LEVIS. [*To himself*] Rats!

CURTAIN

ACT II

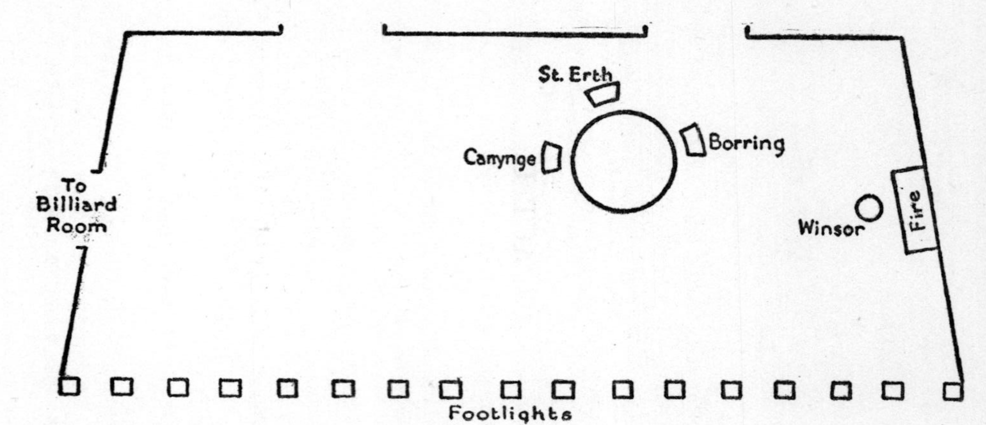

To
Billiard
Room
St. Erth
Canynge
Borring
Winsor
Fire
Footlights

ACT II

SCENE I

Afternoon, three weeks later, in the card room of a London Club. A fire is burning, Left. A door, Right, leads to the billiard-room. Rather Left of Centre, at a card table, LORD ST ERTH, *an old John Bull, sits facing the audience; to his right is* GENERAL CANYNGE, *to his left* AUGUSTUS BORRING, *an essential Clubman, about thirty-five years old, with a very slight and rather becoming stammer or click in his speech. The fourth Bridge player,* CHARLES WINSOR, *stands with his back to the fire.*

BORRING. And the r-rub.

WINSOR. By George! You do hold cards, Borring.

ST ERTH. [*Who has lost*] Not a patch on the old whist—this game. Don't know why I play it—never did.

CANYNGE. St Erth, shall we raise the flag for whist again?

WINSOR. No go, General. You can't go back on pace. No getting a man to walk when he knows he can fly. The young men won't look at it.

BORRING. Better develop it so that t-two can sit out, General.

ST ERTH. We ought to have stuck to the old game. Wish I'd gone to Newmarket, Canynge, in spite of the weather.

CANYNGE. [*Looking at his watch*] Let's hear what's won the Cambridgeshire. Ring, won't you, Winsor?

WINSOR *rings.*

ST ERTH. By the way, Canynge, young De Levis was blackballed.

CANYNGE. What!

ST ERTH. I looked in on my way down.

CANYNGE *sits very still, and* WINSOR *utters a disturbed sound.*

BORRING. But of c-course he was, General. What did you expect?

A FOOTMAN *enters.*

FOOTMAN. Yes, my lord?

ST ERTH. What won the Cambridgeshire?

FOOTMAN. Rosemary, my lord. Sherbet second; Barbizon third. Nine to one the winner.

WINSOR. Thank you. That's all.

FOOTMAN *goes.*

BORRING. Rosemary! And De Levis sold her! But he got a good p-price, I suppose.

The other three look at him.

ST ERTH. Many a slip between price and pocket, young man.

CANYNGE. Cut! [*They cut*].

BORRING. I say, is that the yarn that's going round about his having had a lot of m-money stolen in a country house? By Jove! He'll be pretty s-sick.

WINSOR. You and I, Borring.

He sits down in CANYNGE'S *chair, and the* GENERAL *takes his place by the fire.*

BORRING. Phew! Won't Dancy be mad! He gave that filly away to save her keep. He was rather pleased to find somebody who'd take her. Kentman must have won a p-pot. She was at thirty-threes a fortnight ago.

ST ERTH. All the money goes to fellows who don't know a horse from a haystack.

CANYNGE. [*Profoundly*] And care less. Yes! We want men racing to whom a horse means something.

BORRING. I thought the horse m-meant the same to everyone, General—chance to get the b-better of one's neighbour.

CANYNGE. [*With feeling*] The horse is a noble animal, sir, as you'd know if you'd owed your life to them as often as I have.

BORRING. They always try to *take* mine, General. I shall never belong to the noble f-fellowship of the horse.

ST ERTH. [*Drily*] Evidently. Deal!

As BORRING *begins to deal the door is opened and* MAJOR COLFORD *appears — a lean and moustached cavalryman.*

BORRING. Hallo, C-Colford.

COLFORD. General!

Something in the tone of his voice brings them all to a standstill.

COLFORD. I want your advice. Young De Levis in there [*He points to the billiard-room from which he has just come*] has started a blasphemous story——

CANYNGE. One moment. Mr Borring, d'you mind——

COLFORD. It makes no odds, General. Four of us in there heard him. He's saying it was Ronald Dancy robbed him down at Winsor's. The fellow's mad over losing the price of that filly now she's won the Cambridgeshire.

BORRING. [*All ears*] Dancy! Great S-Scott!

COLFORD. Dancy's in the Club. If he hadn't been I'd have taken it on myself to wring the bounder's neck.

WINSOR *and* BORRING *have risen.* ST ERTH *alone remains seated.*

CANYNGE. [*After consulting* ST ERTH *with a look*] Ask De Levis to be good enough to come in here. Borring, you might see that Dancy doesn't leave the Club. We shall want him. Don't say anything to him, and use your tact to keep people off.

BORRING *goes out, followed by* COLFORD.

WINSOR. Result of hearing he was blackballed—pretty slippy.

CANYNGE. St Erth, I told you there was good reason when I asked you to back young De Levis. Winsor and I knew of this insinuation; I wanted to keep his tongue quiet. It's just wild assertion; to have it bandied about was unfair to Dancy. The duel used to keep people's tongues in order.

ST ERTH. H'm! It never settled anything, except who could shoot straightest.

COLFORD. [*Reappearing*] De Levis says he's nothing to add to what he said to you before, on the subject.

CANYNGE. Kindly tell him that if he wishes to remain a member of this Club he must account to the Committee for such a charge against a fellow-member. Four of us are here, and form a quorum.

COLFORD *goes out again.*

ST ERTH. Did Kentman ever give the police the numbers of those notes, Winsor?

WINSOR. He only had the numbers of two—the hundred, and one of the fifties.

ST ERTH. And they haven't traced 'em?

WINSOR. Not yet.

As he speaks, DE LEVIS *comes in. He is in a highly-coloured, not to say excited state.* COLFORD *follows him.*

DE LEVIS. Well, General Canynge! It's a little too strong all this—a little too strong. [*Under emotion his voice is slightly more exotic*].

CANYNGE. [*Calmly*] It is obvious, Mr De Levis, that you and Captain Dancy can't both remain members of this Club. We ask you for an explanation before requesting one resignation or the other.

DE LEVIS. You've let me down.

CANYNGE. What!

DE LEVIS. Well, I shall tell people that you and Lord St Erth backed me up for one Club, and asked me to resign from another.

CANYNGE. It's a matter of indifference to me, sir, what you tell people.

ST ERTH. [*Drily*] You seem a venomous young man.

DE LEVIS. I'll tell you what seems to me venomous, my lord—chasing a man like a pack of hounds because he isn't your breed.

CANYNGE. You appear to have your breed on the brain, sir. Nobody else does, so far as I know.

DE LEVIS. Suppose I had robbed Dancy, would you chase him out for complaining of it?

COLFORD. My God! If you repeat that——

CANYNGE. Steady, Colford!

WINSOR. You make this accusation that Dancy stole your money in my house on no proof—no proof; and you expect Dancy's friends to treat you as if you were a gentleman! That's too strong, if you like!

DE LEVIS. No proof? Kentman told me at Newmarket yesterday that Dancy *did* know of the sale. He told Goole, and Goole says that he himself spoke of it to Dancy.

WINSOR. Well—if he did?

DE LEVIS. Dancy told you he *didn't* know of it in General Canynge's presence, and mine. [*To* CANYNGE] You can't deny that, if you want to.

CANYNGE. Choose your expressions more nicely, please!

DE LEVIS. Proof! Did they find any footmarks in the grounds below that torn creeper? Not a sign! You saw how he can jump; he won ten pounds from me that same evening betting on what he knew was a certainty. That's your Dancy—a common sharper!

CANYNGE. [*Nodding towards the billiard-room*] Are those fellows still in there, Colford?

COLFORD. Yes.

CANYNGE. Then bring Dancy up, will you? But don't say anything to him.

COLFORD. [*To* DE LEVIS] You may think yourself damned lucky if he doesn't break your neck.

He goes out. The three who are left with DE LEVIS *avert their eyes from him.*

DE LEVIS. [*Smouldering*] I have a memory, and a sting too. Yes, my lord—since you are good enough to call me venomous. [*To* CANYNGE] I quite understand—I'm marked for Coventry now, whatever happens. Well, I'll take Dancy with me.

ST ERTH. [*To himself*] This Club has always had a decent, quiet name.

WINSOR. Are you going to retract, and apologise in front of Dancy and the members who heard you?

DE LEVIS. No fear!

ST ERTH. You must be a very rich man, sir. A jury is likely to take the view that money can hardly compensate for an accusation of that sort.

DE LEVIS *stands silent.*

CANYNGE. Courts of law require proof.

ST ERTH. He can make it a criminal action.

WINSOR. Unless you stop this at once, you may find yourself in prison. *If* you can stop it, that is.

ST ERTH. If I were young Dancy, nothing should induce me.

De Levis. But you didn't steal my money, Lord St Erth.

St Erth. You're deuced positive, sir. So far as I could understand it, there were a dozen ways you could have been robbed. It seems to me you value other men's reputations very lightly.

De Levis. Confront me with Dancy and give me fair play.

Winsor. [*Aside to* Canynge] Is it fair to Dancy not to let him know?

Canynge. Our duty is to the Club now, Winsor. We must have this cleared up.

Colford *comes in, followed by* Borring *and* Dancy.

St Erth. Captain Dancy, a serious accusation has been made against you by this gentleman in the presence of several members of the Club.

Dancy. What is it?

St Erth. That you robbed him of that money at Winsor's.

Dancy. [*Hard and tense*] Indeed! On what grounds is he good enough to say that?

De Levis. [*Tense too*] You gave me that filly to save yourself her keep, and you've been mad about it ever since; you knew from Goole that I had sold her to Kentman and been paid in cash, yet I heard you myself deny that you knew it. You had the next room to me, and you can jump like a cat, as we saw that evening; I found some creepers crushed by a weight on my balcony on that side. When I went to the bath your door was open, and when I came back it was shut.

CANYNGE. That's the first we have heard about the door.

DE LEVIS. I remembered it afterwards.

ST ERTH. Well, Dancy?

DANCY. [*With intense deliberation*] I'll settle this matter with any weapons, when and where he likes.

ST ERTH. [*Drily*] It can't be settled that way—you know very well. You must take it to the Courts, unless he retracts.

DANCY. Will you retract?

DE LEVIS. Why did you tell General Canynge you didn't know Kentman had paid me in cash?

DANCY. Because I didn't.

DE LEVIS. Then Kentman and Goole lied—for no reason?

DANCY. That's nothing to do with me.

DE LEVIS. If you were downstairs all the time, as you say, why was your door first open and then shut?

DANCY. Being downstairs, how should I know? The wind, probably.

DE LEVIS. I should like to hear what your wife says about it.

DANCY. Leave my wife alone, you damned Jew!

ST ERTH. Captain Dancy!

DE LEVIS. [*White with rage*] Thief!

DANCY. Will you fight?

DE LEVIS. You're very smart—dead men tell no tales. No! Bring your action, and we shall see.

DANCY *takes a step towards him, but* CANYNGE *and* WINSOR *interpose.*

ST ERTH. That'll do, Mr De Levis; we won't keep you. [*He looks round*] Kindly consider your membership suspended till this matter has been threshed out.

DE LEVIS. [*Tremulous with anger*] Don't trouble yourselves about my membership. I resign it. [*To* DANCY] You called me a damned Jew. My race was old when you were all savages. I am proud to be a Jew. *Au revoir*, in the Courts.

He goes out, and silence follows his departure.

ST ERTH. Well, Captain Dancy?

DANCY. If the brute won't fight, what am I to do, sir?

ST ERTH. We've told you—take action, to clear your name.

DANCY. Colford, you saw me in the hall writing letters after our game.

COLFORD. Certainly I did; you were there when I went to the smoking-room.

CANYNGE. How long after you left the billiard-room?

COLFORD. About five minutes.

DANCY. It's impossible for me to prove that I was there all the time.

CANYNGE. It's for De Levis to prove what he asserts. You heard what he said about Goole?

DANCY. If he told me, I didn't take it in.

ST ERTH. This concerns the honour of the Club. Are you going to take action?

DANCY. [*Slowly*] That is a very expensive business, Lord St Erth, and I'm hard up. I must think it over. [*He looks round from face to face*] Am I to take it that there is a doubt in your minds, gentlemen?

COLFORD. [*Emphatically*] No.

CANYNGE. That's not the question, Dancy. This accusation was overheard by various members, and we represent the Club. If you don't take action, judgment will naturally go by default.

DANCY. I might prefer to look on the whole thing as beneath contempt.

He turns and goes out. When he is gone there is an even longer silence than after DE LEVIS'S *departure.*

ST ERTH. [*Abruptly*] I don't like it.

WINSOR. I've known him all his life.

COLFORD. You may have my head if he did it, Lord St Erth. He and I have been in too many holes together. By Gad! My toe itches for that fellow's butt end.

BORRING. I'm sorry; but has he t-taken it in quite the right way? I should have thought—hearing it s-suddenly——

COLFORD. Bosh!

WINSOR. It's perfectly damnable for him.

ST ERTH. More damnable if he did it, Winsor.

BORRING. The Courts are b-beastly distrustful, don't you know.

COLFORD. His word's good enough for me.

CANYNGE. We're as anxious to believe Dancy as you, Colford, for the honour of the Army and the Club.

WINSOR. Of course, he'll bring a case, when he's thought it over.

ST ERTH. What are we to do in the meantime?

COLFORD. If Dancy's asked to resign, you may take my resignation too.

BORRING. I thought his wanting to f-fight him a bit screeny.

COLFORD. Wouldn't you have wanted a shot at the brute? A law court? Pah!

WINSOR. Yes. What'll be his position even if he wins?

BORRING. Damages, and a stain on his c-character.

WINSOR. Quite so, unless they find the real thief. People always believe the worst.

COLFORD. [*Glaring at* BORRING] They do.

CANYNGE. There *is* no decent way out of a thing of this sort.

ST ERTH. No. [*Rising*] It leaves a bad taste. I'm sorry for young Mrs Dancy—poor woman!

BORRING. Are you going to play any more?

ST ERTH. [*Abruptly*] No, sir. Good night to you. Canynge, can I give you a lift?

He goes out, followed by CANYNGE.

BORRING. [*After a slight pause*] Well, I shall go and take the t-temperature of the Club.

He goes out.

COLFORD. Damn that effeminate stammering chap! What can we do for Dancy, Winsor?

WINSOR. Colford! [*A slight pause*] The General felt his coat sleeve that night, and it was wet.

COLFORD. Well! What proof's that? No, by

George! An old school-fellow, a brother officer, and a pal.

WINSOR. If he did do it——

COLFORD. He didn't. But if he did, I stick to him, and see him through it, if I could.

WINSOR *walks over to the fire, stares into it, turns round and stares at* COLFORD, *who is standing motionless.*

COLFORD. Yes, by God!

CURTAIN.

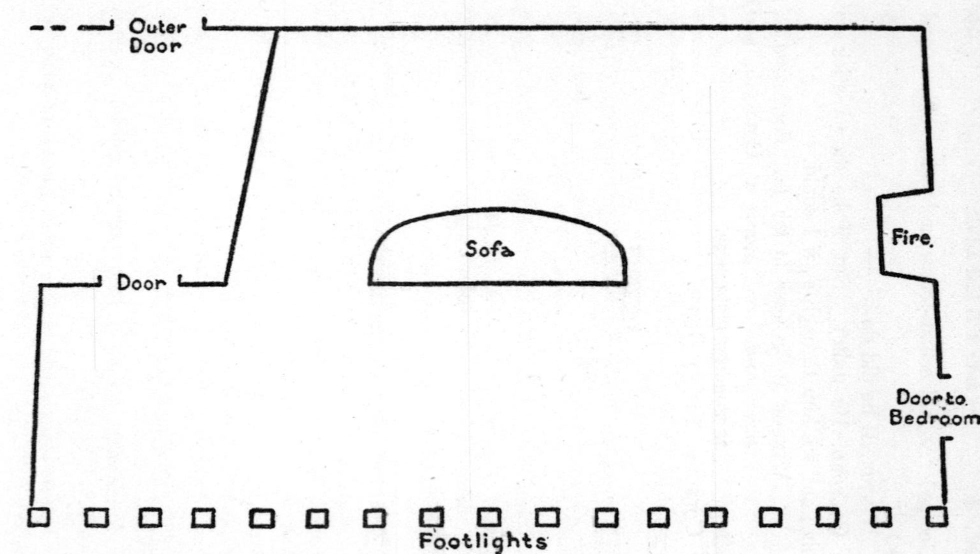

Outer Door
Door
Sofa
Fire.
Door to Bedroom
Footlights

SCENE II *

Morning of the following day. The DANCYS' *flat. In the sitting-room of this small abode* MABEL DANCY *and* MARGARET ORME *are sitting full face to the audience, on a couch in the centre of the room, in front of the imaginary window. There is a fireplace, Left, with fire burning; a door below it, Left; and a door on the Right, facing the audience, leads to a corridor and the outer door of the flat, which is visible. Their voices are heard in rapid exchange; then as the curtain rises, so does* MABEL.

MABEL. But it's monstrous!

MARGARET. Of course! [*She lights a cigarette and hands the case to* MABEL, *who, however, sees nothing but her own thoughts*] De Levis might just as well have pitched on me, except that I can't jump more than six inches in these skirts.

MABEL. It's wicked! Yesterday afternoon at the Club, did you say? Ronny hasn't said a word to me. Why?

MARGARET. [*With a long puff of smoke*] Doesn't want you bothered.

* NOTE.—This should be a small set capable of being set quickly within that of the previous scene.

MABEL. But—— Good heavens!—— Me!

MARGARET. Haven't you found out, Mabel, that he isn't exactly communicative? No desperate character is.

MABEL. Ronny?

MARGARET. Gracious! Wives *are* at a disadvantage, especially early on. You've never hunted with him, my dear. I have. He takes more sudden decisions than any man I ever knew. He's taking one now, I'll bet.

MABEL. That beast, De Levis! I was in our room next door all the time.

MARGARET. Was the door into Ronny's dressing-room open?

MABEL. I don't know; I—I think it was.

MARGARET. Well, you can say so in Court anyway. Not that it matters. Wives are liars by law.

MABEL. [*Staring down at her*] What do you mean —Court?

MARGARET. My dear, he'll have to bring an action for defamation of character, or whatever they call it.

MABEL. Were they talking of this last night at the Winsors'?

MARGARET. Well, you know a dinner-table, Mabel —Scandal is heaven-sent at this time of year.

MABEL. It's terrible, such a thing—terrible!

MARGARET. [*Gloomily*] If only Ronny weren't known to be so broke.

MABEL. [*With her hands to her forehead*] I can't realise—I simply can't. If there's a case would it be all right afterwards?

MARGARET. Do you remember St Offert—cards? No, you wouldn't—you were in high frocks. Well, St Offert got damages, but he also got the hoof, underneath. He lives in Ireland. There isn't the slightest connection, so far as I can see, Mabel, between innocence and reputation. Look at me!

MABEL. We'll fight it tooth and nail!

MARGARET. Mabel, you're pure wool, right through; everybody's sorry for you.

MABEL. It's for *him* they ought——

MARGARET. [*Again handing the cigarette-case*] Do smoke, old thing.

MABEL *takes a cigarette this time, but does not light it.*

It isn't altogether simple. General Canynge was there last night. You don't mind my being beastly frank, do you?

MABEL. No. I want it.

MARGARET. Well, he's all for *esprit de corps* and that. But he was awfully silent.

MABEL. I hate half-hearted friends. Loyalty comes before everything.

MARGARET. Ye-es; but loyalties cut up against each other sometimes, you know.

MABEL. I *must* see Ronny. D'you mind if I go and try to get him on the telephone?

MARGARET. Rather not.

MABEL *goes out by the door Left.*

Poor kid!

She curls herself into a corner of the sofa, as if trying to get away from life. The bell rings. MARGARET *stirs, gets up, and goes out into the corridor, where she opens the door to* LADY ADELA WINSOR, *whom she precedes into the sitting-room.*

Enter the second murderer! D'you know that child knew nothing?

LADY A. Where is she?

MARGARET. Telephoning. Adela, if there's going to be an action, we shall be witnesses. I shall wear black georgette with an écru hat. Have you ever given evidence?

LADY A. Never.

MARGARET. It must be too frightfully thrilling.

LADY A. Oh! Why did I ever ask that wretch De Levis? I used to think him pathetic. Meg—did you know—— Ronald Dancy's coat was wet? The General happened to feel it.

MARGARET. So that's why he was so silent.

LADY A. Yes; and after the scene in the Club yesterday he went to see those bookmakers, and Goole—what a name!—is sure he told Dancy about the sale.

MARGARET. [*Suddenly*] I don't care. He's my third cousin. Don't you feel you *couldn't*, Adela?

LADY A. Couldn't—what?

MARGARET. Stand for De Levis against one of ourselves?

LADY A. That's very narrow, Meg.

MARGARET. Oh! I know lots of splendid Jews, and I rather liked little Ferdy; but when it comes to the point——! *They* all stick together; why shouldn't we? It's in the blood. Open your jugular, and see if you haven't got it.

LADY A. My dear, my great grandmother was a Jewess. I'm very proud of her.

MARGARET. Inoculated. [*Stretching herself*] Prejudices, Adela—or are they loyalties—I don't know—criss-cross—we all cut each other's throats from the best of motives.

LADY A. Oh! I shall remember that. Delightful! [*Holding up a finger*] You got it from Bergson, Meg. Isn't he wonderful?

MARGARET. Yes; have you ever read him?

LADY A. Well—No. [*Looking at the bedroom door*] That poor child! I quite agree. I shall tell everybody it's ridiculous. You don't really think Ronald Dancy——?

MARGARET. I don't know, Adela. There are people who simply can't live without danger. I'm rather like that myself. They're all right when they're getting the D.S.O. or shooting man-eaters; but if there's no excitement going, they'll make it—out of sheer craving. I've seen Ronny Dancy do the maddest things for no mortal reason except the risk. He's had a past, you know.

LADY A. Oh! Do tell!

MARGARET. He did splendidly in the war, of course, because it suited him; but—just before—don't you remember—a very queer bit of riding?

LADY A. No.

MARGARET. Most dare-devil thing—but not quite. You must remember—it was awfully talked about.

And then, of course, right up to his marriage—— [*She lights a cigarette.*]

LADY A. Meg, you're very tantalising!

MARGARET. A foreign-looking girl—most plummy. Oh! Ronny's got charm—this Mabel child doesn't know in the least what she's got hold of!

LADY A. But they're so fond of each other!

MARGARET. That's the mistake. The General isn't mentioning the coat, is he?

LADY A. Oh, no! It was only to Charles.

MABEL *returns.*

MARGARET. Did you get him?

MABEL. No; he's not at Tattersall's, nor at the Club.

LADY ADELA *rises and greets her with an air which suggests bereavement.*

LADY A. Nobody's going to believe this, my dear.

MABEL. [*Looking straight at her*] Nobody who does need come here, or trouble to speak to *us* again.

LADY A. That's what I was afraid of; you're going to be defiant. Now don't! Just be perfectly natural.

MABEL. So easy, isn't it? I could kill anybody who believes such a thing.

MARGARET. You'll want a solicitor, Mabel. Go to old Mr Jacob Twisden.

LADY A. Yes; he's so comforting.

MARGARET. He got my pearls back once—without loss of life. A frightfully good fireside manner. Do get him here, Mabel, and have a heart-to-heart talk, all three of you!

MABEL. [*Suddenly*] Listen! There's Ronny!

DANCY *comes in.*

DANCY. [*With a smile*] Very good of you to have come.

MARGARET. Yes. We're just going. Oh! Ronny, this is quite too—— [*But his face dries her up; and sidling past, she goes*].

LADY A. Charles sent his—love—— [*Her voice dwindles on the word, and she, too, goes*].

DANCY. [*Crossing to his wife*] What have they been saying?

MABEL. Ronny! Why didn't you tell me?

DANCY. I wanted to see De Levis again first.

MABEL. That wretch! How dare he? Darling! [*She suddenly clasps and kisses him. He does not return the kiss, but remains rigid in her arms, so that she draws away and looks at him*] It's hurt you awfully, I know.

DANCY. Look here, Mabel! Apart from that muck—this is a ghastly tame-cat sort of life. Let's cut it and get out to Nairobi. I can scare up the money for that.

MABEL. [*Aghast*] But how can we? Everybody would say——

DANCY. Let them! We shan't be here.

MABEL. I couldn't bear people to think——

DANCY. I don't care a damn what people think—monkeys and cats. I never could stand their rotten menagerie. Besides, what does it matter how I act; if I bring an action and get damages—if I pound him to a jelly—it's all no good! I can't *prove* it. There'll be plenty of people unconvinced.

MABEL. But they'll find the real thief.

DANCY. [*With a queer little smile*] Will staying here help them to do that?

MABEL. [*In a sort of agony*] Oh! I couldn't—it looks like running away. We *must* stay and fight it!

DANCY. Suppose I didn't get a verdict—you never can tell.

MABEL. But you must—I was there all the time, with the door open.

DANCY. Was it?

MABEL. I'm almost sure.

DANCY. Yes. But you're my wife.

MABEL. [*Bewildered*] Ronny, I don't understand—suppose I'd been accused of stealing pearls!

DANCY. [*Wincing*] I can't.

MABEL. But I might—just as easily. What would you think of me if I ran away from it?

DANCY. I see. [*A pause*] All right! You shall have a run for your money. I'll go and see old Twisden.

MABEL. Let me come! [DANCY *shakes his head*] Why not? I can't be happy a moment unless I'm fighting this.

DANCY *puts out his hand suddenly and grips hers.*

DANCY. You *are* a little brick!

MABEL. [*Pressing his hand to her breast and looking into his face*] Do you know what Margaret called you?

RONNY. No.

MABEL. A desperate character.

DANCY. Ha! I'm not a tame cat, any more than she.

The bell rings. MABEL *goes out to the door and her voice is heard saying coldly.*

MABEL. Will you wait a minute, please?

Returning.

It's De Levis—to see you. [*In a low voice*] Let me see him alone first. Just for a minute! Do!

DANCY. [*After a moment's silence*] Go ahead!

He goes out into the bedroom.

MABEL. [*Going to the door, Right*] Come in.

DE LEVIS *comes in, and stands embarrassed.*

Yes?

DE LEVIS. [*With a slight bow*] Your husband, Mrs Dancy?

MABEL. He is in. Why do you want to see him?

DE LEVIS. He came round to my rooms just now, when I was out. He threatened me yesterday. I don't choose him to suppose I'm afraid of him.

MABEL. [*With a great and manifest effort at self-control*] Mr De Levis, you are robbing my husband of his good name.

DE LEVIS. [*Sincerely*] I admire your trustfulness, Mrs Dancy.

MABEL. [*Staring at him*] How can you do it? What do you want? What's your motive? You can't possibly believe that my husband is a *thief!*

DE LEVIS. Unfortunately.

MABEL. How dare you? How dare you? Don't you know that I was in our bedroom all the time with the door open? Do you accuse me too?

DE LEVIS. No, Mrs Dancy.

MABEL. But you do. I must have seen, I must have heard.

DE LEVIS. A wife's memory is not very good when her husband is in danger.

MABEL. In other words, I'm lying.

DE LEVIS. No. Your wish is mother to your thought, that's all.

MABEL. [*After staring again with a sort of horror, turns to get control of herself. Then turning back to him*] Mr De Levis, I appeal to you as a gentleman to behave to us as you would we should behave to you. Withdraw this wicked charge, and write an apology that Ronald can show.

DE LEVIS. Mrs Dancy, I am not a gentleman, I am only a—damned Jew. Yesterday I might possibly have withdrawn to spare you. But when my race is insulted I have nothing to say to your husband, but as he wishes to see me, I've come. Please let him know.

MABEL. [*Regarding him again with that look of horror—slowly*] I think what you are doing is too horrible for words.

DE LEVIS *gives her a slight bow, and as he does so* DANCY *comes quickly in, Left. The two men stand with the length of the sofa between them.* MABEL, *behind the sofa, turns her eyes on her husband, who has a paper in his right hand.*

DE LEVIS. You came to see me.

DANCY. Yes. I want you to sign this.

De Levis. I will sign nothing.

Dancy. Let me read it: "I apologise to Captain Dancy for the reckless and monstrous charge I made against him, and I retract every word of it."

De Levis. Not much!

Dancy. You will sign.

De Levis. I tell you this is useless. I will sign nothing. The charge is true; you wouldn't be playing this game if it weren't. I'm going. You'll hardly try violence in the presence of your wife; and if you try it anywhere else—— look out for yourself.

Dancy. Mabel, I want to speak to him alone.

Mabel. No, no!

De Levis. Quite right, Mrs Dancy. Black and tan swashbuckling will only make things worse for him.

Dancy. So you shelter behind a woman, do you, you skulking cur!

De Levis *takes a step, with fists clenched and eyes blazing.* Dancy, *too, stands ready to spring—the moment is cut short by* Mabel *going quickly to her husband.*

Mabel. Don't, Ronny. It's undignified! He isn't worth it.

Dancy *suddenly tears the paper in two, and flings it into the fire.*

Dancy. Get out of here, you swine!

De Levis *stands a moment irresolute, then, turning to the door, he opens it, stands again for a moment with a smile on his face, then goes.* MABEL *crosses swiftly to the door, and shuts it as the outer door closes. Then she stands quite still, looking at her husband—her face expressing a sort of startled suspense.*

DANCY. [*Turning and looking at her*] Well! Do you agree with him?

MABEL. What do you mean?

DANCY. That I wouldn't be playing this game unless——

MABEL. Don't! You hurt me!

DANCY. Yes. You don't know much of me, Mabel.

MABEL. Ronny!

DANCY. What did you say to that swine?

MABEL. [*Her face averted*] That he was robbing *us.* [*Turning to him suddenly*] Ronny—you—didn't? I'd rather know.

DANCY. Ha! I thought that was coming.

MABEL. [*Covering her face*] Oh! How horrible of me—how horrible!

DANCY. Not at all. The thing looks bad.

MABEL. [*Dropping her hands*] If *I* can't believe in you, who can? [*Going to him, throwing her arms round him, and looking up into his face*] Ronny! If all the world—*I'd* believe in you. You know I would.

DANCY. That's all right, Mabs! That's all right! [*His face, above her head, is contorted for a moment, then hardens into a mask*] Well, what shall we do?

MABEL. Oh! Let's go to that lawyer—let's go at once!

DANCY. All right. Get your hat on.

MABEL *passes him, and goes into the bedroom, Left.* DANCY, *left alone, stands quite still, staring before him. With a sudden shrug of his shoulders he moves quickly to his hat and takes it up just as* MABEL *returns, ready to go out. He opens the door; and crossing him, she stops in the doorway, looking up with a clear and trustful gaze as*

The CURTAIN *falls.*

ACT III

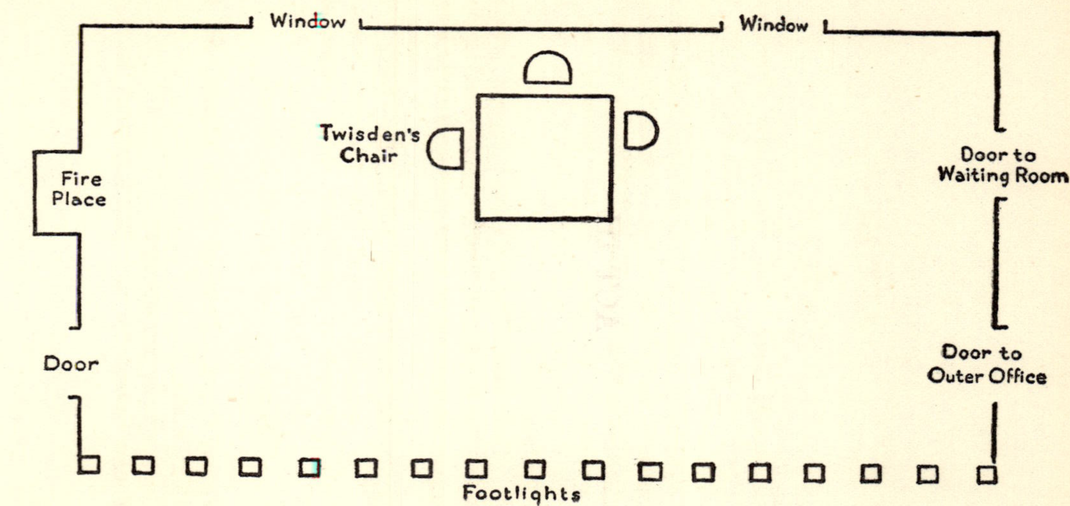
Window
Window
Twisden's Chair
Fire Place
Door to Waiting Room
Door
Door to Outer Office
Footlights

ACT III

SCENE I

Three months later. Old Mr Jacob Twisden's *Room, at the offices of Twisden & Graviter, in Lincoln's Inn Fields, is spacious, with two large windows at back, a fine old fireplace, Right, a door below it, and two doors, Left. Between the windows is a large table sideways to the window wall, with a chair in the middle on the right-hand side, a chair against the wall, and a client's chair on the left-hand side.*

Graviter, Twisden's *much younger partner, is standing in front of the right-hand window looking out on to the Fields, where the lamps are being lighted, and a taxi's engine is running down below. He turns his sanguine, shrewd face from the window towards a grandfather clock, between the doors, Left, which is striking "four." The door, Left Forward, is opened.*

Young Clerk. [*Entering*] A Mr Gilman, sir, to see Mr Twisden.

Graviter. By appointment?

Young Clerk. No, sir. But important, he says.

GRAVITER. I'll see him.

The CLERK *goes.*

GRAVITER *sits right of table. The* CLERK *returns, ushering in an oldish* MAN, *who looks what he is, the proprietor of a large modern grocery store. He wears a dark overcoat and carries a pot hat. His gingery grey moustache and mutton-chop whiskers give him the expression of a cat.*

GRAVITER. [*Sizing up his social standing*] Mr Gilman? Yes.

GILMAN. [*Doubtfully*] Mr Jacob Twisden?

GRAVITER. [*Smiling*] His partner. Graviter my name is.

GILMAN. Mr Twisden's not in, then?

GRAVITER. No. He's at the Courts. They're just up; he should be in directly. But he'll be busy.

GILMAN. Old Mr Jacob Twisden—I've heard of him.

GRAVITER. Most people have.

A pause.

GILMAN. It's this Dancy De Levis case that's keepin' him at the Courts, I suppose?

GRAVITER *nods.*

Won't be finished for a day or two?

GRAVITER *shakes his head.*

No. Astonishin' the interest taken in it.

GRAVITER. As you say.

GILMAN. The Smart Set, eh? This Captain Dancy got the D.S.O., didn't he?

GRAVITER *nods.*

Sad to have a thing like that said about you. I thought he gave his evidence well; and his wife too. Looks as if this De Levis had got some private spite. *Searchy la femme*, I said to Mrs Gilman only this morning, before I——

GRAVITER. By the way, sir, what is your business?

GILMAN. Well, my business here—— No, if you'll excuse me, I'd rather wait and see old Mr Jacob Twisden. It's delicate, and I'd like his experience.

GRAVITER. [*With a shrug*] Very well; then, perhaps, you'll go in there. [*He moves towards the door, Left Back*].

GILMAN. Thank you. [*Following*] You see, I've never been mixed up with the law——

GRAVITER. [*Opening the door*] No?

GILMAN. And I don't want to begin. When you do, you don't know where you'll stop, do you? You see, I've only come from a sense of duty; and —other reasons.

GRAVITER. Not uncommon.

GILMAN. [*Producing card*] This is my card. Gilman's—several branches, but this is the 'ead.

GRAVITER. [*Scrutinising card*] Exactly.

GILMAN. Grocery—I daresay you know me; or your wife does. They say old Mr Jacob Twisden refused a knighthood. If it's not a rude question, why was that?

GRAVITER. Ask him, sir; ask him.

GILMAN. I said to my wife at the time, "He's holdin' out for a baronetcy."

GRAVITER *closes the door with an exasperated smile.*

YOUNG CLERK. [*Opening the door, Left Forward*] Mr Winsor, sir, and Miss Orme.

They enter, and the CLERK *withdraws.*

GRAVITER. How d'you do, Miss Orme? How do you do, Winsor?

WINSOR. Twisden not back, Graviter?

GRAVITER. Not yet.

WINSOR. Well, they've got through De Levis's witnesses. Sir Frederic was at the very top of his form. It's looking quite well. But I hear they've just subpœnaed Canynge after all. His evidence is to be taken to-morrow.

GRAVITER. Oho!

WINSOR. I said Dancy ought to have called him.

GRAVITER. We considered it. Sir Frederic decided that he could use him better in cross-examination.

WINSOR. Well! I don't know that. Can I go and see him before he gives evidence to-morrow?

GRAVITER. I should like to hear Mr Jacob on that, Winsor. He'll be in directly.

WINSOR. They had Kentman, and Goole, the Inspector, the other bobby, my footman, Dancy's banker, and his tailor.

GRAVITER. Did we shake Kentman or Goole?

WINSOR. Very little. Oh! by the way, the numbers of those two notes were given, and I see they're published in the evening papers. I suppose the police wanted that. I tell you what I find,

Graviter—a general feeling that there's something behind it all that doesn't come out.

GRAVITER. The public wants its money's worth —always does in these Society cases; they brew so long beforehand, you see.

WINSOR. They're looking for something lurid.

MARGARET. When I was in the box, I thought they were looking for me. [*Taking out her cigarette case*] I suppose I mustn't smoke, Mr Graviter?

GRAVITER. Do!

MARGARET. Won't Mr Jacob have a fit?

GRAVITER. Yes, but not till you've gone.

MARGARET. Just a whiff. [*She lights a cigarette*].

WINSOR. [*Suddenly*] It's becoming a sort of Dreyfus case—people taking sides quite outside the evidence.

MARGARET. There are more of the chosen in Court every day. Mr Graviter, have you noticed the two on the jury?

GRAVITER. [*With a smile*] No; I can't say——

MARGARET. Oh! but quite distinctly. Don't you think they ought to have been challenged?

GRAVITER. De Levis might have challenged the other ten, Miss Orme.

MARGARET. Dear me, now! I never thought of that.

As she speaks, the door Left Forward is opened and old MR JACOB TWISDEN *comes in. He is tallish and narrow, sixty-eight years old, grey, with narrow little whiskers curling round his narrow ears, and a narrow bow ribbon curling round his collar. He wears a long, narrow-tailed coat, and strapped trousers on his narrow legs. His nose and face are narrow, shrewd, and kindly. He has a way of narrowing his shrewd and kindly eyes. His nose is seen to twitch and sniff.*

TWISDEN. Ah! How are you, Charles? How do you do, my dear?

MARGARET. Dear Mr Jacob, I'm smoking. Isn't it disgusting? But they don't allow it in Court, you know. Such a pity! The Judge might have a hookah. Oh! wouldn't he look sweet—the darling!

TWISDEN. [*With a little, old-fashioned bow*] It does not become everybody as it becomes you, Margaret.

MARGARET. Mr Jacob, how charming! [*With a slight grimace she puts out her cigarette*].

GRAVITER. Man called Gilman waiting in there to see you specially.

TWISDEN. Directly. Turn up the light, would you, Graviter?

GRAVITER. [*Turning up the light*] Excuse me.

He goes.

WINSOR. Look here, Mr Twisden——

TWISDEN. Sit down; sit down, my dear.

And he himself sits behind the table, as a cup of tea is brought in to him by the YOUNG CLERK, *with two Marie biscuits in the saucer.*

Will you have some, Margaret?

MARGARET. No, dear Mr Jacob.

TWISDEN. Charles?

WINSOR. No, thanks.

The door is closed.

TWISDEN. [*Dipping a biscuit in the tea*] Now, then?

WINSOR. The General knows something which on the face of it looks rather queer. Now that he's going to be called, oughtn't Dancy to be told of it, so that he may be ready with his explanation, in case it comes out?

TWISDEN. [*Pouring some tea into the saucer*] Without knowing, I can't tell you.

WINSOR *and* MARGARET *exchange looks, and* TWISDEN *drinks from the saucer.*

MARGARET. Tell him, Charles.

WINSOR. Well! It rained that evening at Meldon. The General happened to put his hand on Dancy's shoulder, and it was damp.

TWISDEN *puts the saucer down and replaces the cup in it. They both look intently at him.*

TWISDEN. I take it that General Canynge won't say anything he's not compelled to say.

MARGARET. No, of course; but, Mr Jacob, they might ask; they know it rained. And he is such a George Washington.

TWISDEN. [*Toying with a pair of tortoise-shell glasses*] They didn't ask either of *you*. Still—no harm in your telling Dancy.

WINSOR. I'd rather *you* did it, Margaret.

MARGARET. I daresay. [*She mechanically takes*

out her cigarette-case, catches the lift of TWISDEN'S *eyebrows, and puts it back*].

WINSOR. Well, we'll go together. I don't want Mrs Dancy to hear.

MARGARET. Do tell me, Mr Jacob; is he going to win?

TWISDEN. I think so, Margaret; I think so.

MARGARET. It'll be too frightful if he doesn't get a verdict, after all this. But I don't know what we shall do when it's over. I've been sitting in that Court all these three days, watching, and it's made me feel there's nothing we like better than seeing people skinned. Well, bye-bye, bless you!

TWISDEN *rises and pats her hand.*

WINSOR. Half a second, Margaret. Wait for me.

She nods and goes out.

Mr Twisden, what do you really think?

TWISDEN. I am Dancy's lawyer, my dear Charles, as well as yours.

WINSOR. Well, can I go and see Canynge?

TWISDEN. Better not.

WINSOR. If they get that out of him, and recall me, am I to say he told me of it at the time?

TWISDEN. You didn't feel the coat yourself? And Dancy wasn't present? Then what Canynge told you is not evidence. *We'll* stop your being asked.

WINSOR. Thank goodness. Good-bye!

WINSOR *goes out.*

TWISDEN, *behind his table, motionless, taps his teeth with the eyeglasses in his narrow, well-kept hand. After a long shake of his head and a shrug of his rather high shoulders he sniffs, goes to the window and opens it. Then crossing to the door, Left Back, he throws it open and says:*

TWISDEN. At your service, sir.

GILMAN *comes forth, nursing his pot hat.*

Be seated.

TWISDEN *closes the window behind him, and takes his seat.*

GILMAN. [*Taking the client's chair, to the left of the table*] Mr Twisden, I believe? My name's Gilman, head of Gilman's Department Stores. You have my card.

TWISDEN. [*Looking at the card*] Yes. What can we do for you?

GILMAN. Well, I've come to you from a sense of duty, sir, and also a feelin' of embarrassment. [*He takes from his breast pocket an evening paper*] You see, I've been followin' this Dancy case—it's a good deal talked of in Putney—and I read this at half-past two this afternoon. To be precise, at 2.25. [*He rises and hands the paper to* TWISDEN, *and with a thick gloved forefinger indicates a passage*] When I read these numbers, I 'appened to remember givin' change for a fifty-pound note—don't often 'ave one in, you know—so I went to the cash-box out of curiosity, to see that I 'adn't got it. Well, I 'ad; and here it is. [*He draws out from his breast pocket and lays before* TWISDEN *a fifty-pound banknote*] It was brought in to change by a customer of mine three days ago, and he got value for it. Now, that's a stolen note, it seems, and you'd like to know what I did. Mind you, that customer of mine I've known 'im—well—eight or nine years; an Italian he is—wine salesman, and so far's I know, a respectable man—foreign-lookin', but nothin' more. Now, this was at 'alf-past two, and I was at my head branch at Putney, where I live. I want you to mark the time, so as you'll see I 'aven't wasted a minute. I took a cab and I drove straight to my customer's private residence in Putney, where he lives with his daughter—Ricardos his name is, Paolio Ricardos. They tell me there that he's at his business shop in the City. So off I go in the cab again, and there I find him. Well, sir, I showed this paper to him and I produced the note. "Here," I said, "you brought this to me and you got value for it." Well, that man was taken aback. If I'm a judge, Mr Twisden, he was taken aback, not to speak in a guilty way, but he was, as you might say, flummoxed. "Now," I said to him, "where did you get it—that's the point?" He took his time to answer, and then he said: "Well, Mr Gilman," he said, "you know me; I am an honourable man. I can't tell you offhand, but I am above the board." He's foreign, you know, in his expressions. "Yes," I said, "that's all very well," I said, "but here I've got a stolen note and you've got the value for it. Now I tell you," I said, "what I'm going to do; I'm going straight with this note to Mr Jacob Twisden, who's got this Dancy De Levis case in 'and. He's a well-known Society lawyer," I said, "of great experience." "Oh!" he said, "that is what you do?"—funny the way he speaks! "Then I come with you!"—And I've got him in the cab below. I want to tell you everything before he comes up. On the way I tried to get something out of him, but I couldn't—I could *not.* "This is very awkward," I said at last. "It is, Mr Gilman," was his reply; and he began to talk about his Sicilian claret—a very good wine, mind you; but under the circumstances it seemed to me uncalled for. Have I made it clear to you?

TWISDEN. [*Who has listened with extreme attention*] Perfectly, Mr Gilman. I'll send down for him. [*He touches a hand-bell*].

The YOUNG CLERK *appears at the door, Left Forward.*

A gentleman in a taxi—waiting. Ask him to be so good as to step up. Oh! and send Mr Graviter here again.

The YOUNG CLERK *goes out.*

GILMAN. As I told you, sir, I've been followin' this case. It's what you might call piquant. And I should be very glad if it came about that this helped Captain Dancy. I take an interest, because, to tell you the truth, [*Confidentially*] I don't like—well, not to put too fine a point upon it—'Ebrews. They work harder; they're more sober; they're honest; and they're everywhere. I've nothing against them, but the fact is—they get *on* so.

TWISDEN. [*Cocking an eye*] A thorn in the flesh, Mr Gilman.

GILMAN. Well, I prefer my own countrymen, and that's the truth of it.

As he speaks, GRAVITER *comes in by the door Left Forward.*

TWISDEN. [*Pointing to the newspaper and the note*] Mr Gilman has brought this, of which he is holder for value. His customer, who changed it three days ago, is coming up.

GRAVITER. The fifty-pounder. I see. [*His face is long and reflective*].

YOUNG CLERK. [*Entering*] Mr Ricardos, sir.

He goes out.

RICARDOS *is a personable, Italian-looking man in a frock coat, with a dark moustachioed face and dark hair a little grizzled. He looks anxious, and bows.*

TWISDEN. Mr Ricardos? My name is Jacob Twisden. My partner. [*Holding up a finger, as* RICARDOS *would speak*] Mr Gilman has told us about this note. You took it to him, he says, three days ago; that is, on Monday, and received cash for it?

RICARDOS. Yes, sare.

TWISDEN. You were *not* aware that it was stolen?

RICARDOS. [*With his hand to his breast*] Oh! no, sare.

TWISDEN. You received it from——?

RICARDOS. A minute, sare; I would weesh to explain—— [*With an expressive shrug*] in private.

TWISDEN. [*Nodding*] Mr Gilman, your conduct has been most prompt. You may safely leave the matter in our hands, now. Kindly let us retain this note; and ask for my cashier as you go out and give him [*He writes*] this. He will reimburse you. We will take any necessary steps ourselves.

GILMAN. [*In slight surprise, with modest pride*] Well, sir, I'm in your 'ands. I must be guided by you, with your experience. I'm glad you think I acted rightly.

TWISDEN. Very rightly, Mr Gilman—very rightly. [*Rising*] Good-afternoon!

GILMAN. Good-afternoon, sir. Good-afternoon, gentlemen! [*To* TWISDEN] I'm sure I'm very 'appy to have made your acquaintance, sir. It's a well-known name.

TWISDEN. Thank you.

GILMAN *retreats, glances at* RICARDOS, *and turns again.*

GILMAN. I suppose there's nothing else I ought to do, in the interests of the law? I'm a careful man.

TWISDEN. If there is, Mr Gilman, we will let you know. We have your address. You may make your mind easy; but don't speak of this. It might interfere with Justice.

GILMAN. Oh! I shouldn't dream of it. I've no wish to be mixed up in anything conspicuous. That's not my principle at all. Good-day, gentlemen.

He goes.

TWISDEN. [*Seating himself*] Now, sir, will you sit down.

But RICARDOS *does not sit; he stands looking uneasily across the table at* GRAVITER.

You may speak out.

RICARDOS. Well, Mr Tweesden and sare, this matter is very serious for me, and very delicate—it concairns my honour. I am in a great difficulty.

TWISDEN. When in difficulty—complete frankness, sir.

RICARDOS. It is a family matter, sare, I——

TWISDEN. Let me be frank with you. [*Telling his points off on his fingers*] We have your admission that you changed this stopped note for value. It will be our duty to inform the Bank of England that it has been traced to you. You will have to account to them for your possession of it. I suggest to you that it will be far better to account frankly to us.

RICARDOS. [*Taking out a handkerchief and quite openly wiping his hands and forehead*] I received this note, sare, with others, from a gentleman, sare, in settlement of a debt of honour, and I know nothing of where he got them.

TWISDEN. H'm! that is very vague. If that is all you can tell us, I'm afraid——

RICARDOS. Gentlemen, this is very painful for me. It is my daughter's good name—— [*He again wipes his brow*].

TWISDEN. Come, sir, speak out!

RICARDOS. [*Desperately*] The notes were a settlement to her from this gentleman, of whom she was a great friend.

TWISDEN. [*Suddenly*] I am afraid we must press you for the name of the gentleman.

RICARDOS. Sare, if I give it to you, and it does 'im 'arm, what will my daughter say? This is a bad matter for me. He behaved well to her; and she is attached to him still; sometimes she is crying yet because she lost him. And now we betray him, perhaps, who knows? This is very unpleasant for me. [*Taking up the paper*] Here it gives the number of another note—a 'undred-pound note. I 'ave that too. [*He takes a note from his breast pocket*].

GRAVITER. How much did he give you in all?

RICARDOS. For my daughter's settlement one thousand pounds. I understand he did not wish to give a cheque because of his marriage. So I did not think anything about it being in notes, you see.

TWISDEN. When did he give you this money?

RICARDOS. The middle of Octobare last.

TWISDEN. [*Suddenly looking up*] Mr Ricardos, was it Captain Dancy?

RICARDOS. [*Again wiping his forehead*] Gentlemen, I am so fond of my daughter. I have only the one, and no wife.

TWISDEN. [*With an effort*] Yes, yes; but I must know.

RICARDOS. Sare, if I tell you, will you give me your good word that my daughter shall not hear of it?

TWISDEN. So far as we are able to prevent it—certainly.

RICARDOS. Sare, I trust you.—It was Captain Dancy.

A long pause.

GRAVITER. [*Suddenly*] Were you blackmailing him?

TWISDEN. [*Holding up his hand*] My partner means, did you press him for this settlement?

RICARDOS. I did think it my duty to my daughter to ask that he make compensation to her.

TWISDEN. With threats that you would tell his wife?

RICARDOS. [*With a shrug*] Captain Dancy was a man of honour. He said: "Of course I will do this." I trusted him. And a month later I did remind him, and he gave me this money for her. I do not know where he got it—I do not know. Gentlemen, I have invested it all on her—every penny—except this note, for which I had the purpose to buy her a necklace. That is the swearéd truth.

TWISDEN. I must keep this note. [*He touches the hundred-pound note*] You will not speak of this to anyone. *I* may recognise that you were a holder for value received—others might take a different view. Good-day, sir. Graviter, see Mr Ricardos out, and take his address.

RICARDOS. [*Pressing his hands over the breast of his frock coat—with a sigh*] Gentlemen, I beg you—remember what I said. [*With a roll of his eyes*] My daughter—I am not happee. Good-day.

He turns and goes out slowly, Left Forward, followed by GRAVITER.

TWISDEN. [*To himself*] Young Dancy! [*He pins the two notes together and places them in an envelope, then stands motionless except for his eyes and hands, which restlessly express the disturbance within him.*

GRAVITER *returns, carefully shuts the door, and going up to him, hands him* RICARDOS' *card.*

[*Looking at the card*] Villa Benvenuto. This will have to be verified, but I'm afraid it's true. That man was not acting.

GRAVITER. What's to be done about Dancy?

TWISDEN. Can you understand a gentleman——?

GRAVITER. I don't know, sir. The war loosened "form" all over the place. I saw plenty of that myself. And some men have no moral sense. From the first I've had doubts.

TWISDEN. We can't go on with the case.

GRAVITER. Phew! . . . [*A moment's silence*] Gosh! It's an awful thing for his wife.

TWISDEN. Yes.

GRAVITER. [*Touching the envelope*] Chance brought this here, sir. That man won't talk—he's too scared.

TWISDEN. Gilman.

GRAVITER. Too respectable. If De Levis got those notes back, and the rest of the money, anonymously?

TWISDEN. But the case, Graviter; the case.

GRAVITER. I don't believe this alters what I've been thinking.

TWISDEN. Thought is one thing—knowledge another. There's duty to our profession. Ours is a fine calling. On the good faith of solicitors a very great deal hangs. [*He crosses to the hearth as if warmth would help him*].

GRAVITER. It'll let him in for a prosecution. He came to us in confidence.

TWISDEN. Not as against the law.

GRAVITER. No. I suppose not. [*A pause*] By Jove, I don't like losing this case. I don't like the admission we backed such a wrong 'un.

TWISDEN. Impossible to go on. Apart from ourselves, there's Sir Frederic. We must disclose to him—can't let him go on in the dark. Complete confidence between solicitor and counsel is the essence of professional honour.

GRAVITER. What are you going to do then, sir?

TWISDEN. See Dancy at once. Get him on the 'phone.

GRAVITER. [*Taking up the telephone*] Get me Captain Dancy's flat. . . . What? . . . [*To* TWISDEN] Mrs Dancy is here. That's *à propos* with a vengeance. Are you going to see her, sir?

TWISDEN. [*After a moment's painful hesitation*] I must.

GRAVITER. [*Telephoning*] Bring Mrs Dancy up. [*He turns to the window*].

MABEL DANCY *is shown in, looking very pale.* TWISDEN *advances from the fire, and takes her hand.*

MABEL. Major Colford's taken Ronny off in his car for the night. I thought it would do him good. I said I'd come round in case there was anything you wanted to say before to-morrow.

TWISDEN. [*Taken aback*] Where have they gone?

MABEL. I don't know, but he'll be home before ten o'clock to-morrow. Is there anything?

TWISDEN. Well, I'd like to see him before the Court sits. Send him on here as soon as he comes.

MABEL. [*With her hand to her forehead*] Oh! Mr Twisden, when will it be over? My head's getting awful sitting in that Court.

TWISDEN. My dear Mrs Dancy, there's no need at all for you to come down to-morrow; take a rest and nurse your head.

MABEL. Really and truly?

TWISDEN. Yes; it's the very best thing you can do.

GRAVITER *turns his head, and looks at them unobserved.*

MABEL. How do you think it's going?

TWISDEN. It went very well to-day; very well indeed.

MABEL. You must be awfully fed up with us.

TWISDEN. My dear young lady, that's our business. [*He takes her hand*].

MABEL'S *face suddenly quivers. She draws her hand away, and covers her lips with it.*

There, there! You want a day off badly.

MABEL. I'm so tired of——! Thank you so much for all you're doing. Good night! Good night, Mr Graviter!

GRAVITER. Good night, Mrs Dancy.

MABEL *goes.*

GRAVITER. D'you know, I believe she knows.

TWISDEN. No, no! She believes in him implicitly. A staunch little woman. Poor thing!

GRAVITER. Hasn't that shaken you, sir? It has me.

TWISDEN. No, no! I—I can't go on with the case. It's breaking faith. Get Sir Frederic's chambers.

GRAVITER. [*Telephoning, and getting a reply, looks round at* TWISDEN] Yes?

TWISDEN. Ask if I can come round and see him.

GRAVITER. [*Telephoning*] Can Sir Frederic spare Mr Twisden a few minutes now if he comes round? [*Receiving reply*] He's gone down to Brighton for the night.

TWISDEN. H'm! What hotel?

GRAVITER. [*Telephoning*] What's his address? What . . .? [*To* TWISDEN] The Bedford.

TWISDEN. I'll go down.

GRAVITER. [*Telephoning*] Thank you. All right. [*He rings off*].

TWISDEN. Just look out the trains down and up early to-morrow.

GRAVITER *takes up an A B C, and* TWISDEN *takes up the Ricardos card.*

TWISDEN. Send to this address in Putney, verify the fact that Ricardos has a daughter, and give me a trunk call to Brighton. Better go yourself, Graviter. If you see her, don't say anything, of course—invent some excuse. [GRAVITER *nods*] I'll be up in time to see Dancy.

GRAVITER. By George! I feel bad about this.

TWISDEN. Yes. But professional honour comes first. What time is that train? [*He bends over the A B C*].

CURTAIN.

SCENE II

The same room on the following morning at ten-twenty-five, by the Grandfather clock.

The YOUNG CLERK *is ushering in* DANCY, *whose face is perceptibly harder than it was three months ago, like that of a man who has lived under great restraint.*

DANCY. He wanted to see me before the Court sat.

YOUNG CLERK. Yes, sir. Mr Twisden will see you in one minute. He had to go out of town last night. [*He prepares to open the waiting-room door*].

DANCY. Were *you* in the war?

YOUNG CLERK. Yes.

DANCY. How can you stick this?

YOUNG CLERK. [*With a smile*] My trouble was to stick that, sir.

DANCY. But you get no excitement from year's end to year's end. It'd drive me mad.

YOUNG CLERK. [*Shyly*] A case like this is pretty exciting. I'd give a lot to see us win it.

DANCY. [*Staring at him*] Why? What is it to you?

YOUNG CLERK. I don't know, sir. It's—it's like football—you want your side to win. [*He opens the waiting-room door. Expanding*] You see some rum starts, too, in a lawyer's office in a quiet way.

DANCY *enters the waiting-room, and the* YOUNG CLERK, *shutting the door, meets* TWISDEN *as he comes in, Left Forward, and takes from him overcoat, top hat, and a small bag.*

YOUNG CLERK. Captain Dancy's waiting, sir. [*He indicates the waiting-room*].

TWISDEN. [*Narrowing his lips*] Very well. Mr Graviter gone to the Courts?

YOUNG CLERK. Yes, sir.

TWISDEN. Did he leave anything for me?

YOUNG CLERK. On the table, sir.

TWISDEN. [*Taking up an envelope*] Thank you.

The CLERK *goes.*

TWISDEN. [*Opening the envelope and reading*] "All corroborates." H'm! [*He puts it in his pocket and takes out of an envelope the two notes, lays them on the table, and covers them with a sheet of blotting-paper; stands a moment preparing himself, then goes to the door of the waiting-room, opens it, and says:*] Now, Captain Dancy. Sorry to have kept you waiting.

DANCY. [*Entering*] Winsor came to me yesterday about General Canynge's evidence. Is that what you wanted to speak to me about?

TWISDEN. No. It isn't that.

DANCY. [*Looking at his wrist watch*] By me it's just on the half-hour, sir.

TWISDEN. Yes. I don't want you to go to the Court.

DANCY. Not?

TWISDEN. I have very serious news for you.

DANCY. [*Wincing and collecting himself*] Oh!

TWISDEN. These two notes. [*He uncovers the notes*] After the Court rose yesterday we had a man called Ricardos here. [*A pause*] Is there any need for me to say more?

DANCY. [*Unflinching*] No. What now?

TWISDEN. Our duty was plain; we could not go on with the case. I have consulted Sir Frederic. He felt—he felt that he must throw up his brief, and he will do that the moment the Court sits. Now I want to talk to you about what you're going to do.

DANCY. That's very good of you, considering.

TWISDEN. I don't pretend to understand, but I imagine you may have done this in a moment of reckless bravado, feeling, perhaps, that as you gave the mare to De Levis, the money was by rights as much yours as his.

Stopping DANCY, *who is about to speak, with a gesture.*

To satisfy a debt of honour to this—lady; and, no doubt, to save your wife from hearing of it from the man Ricardos. Is that so?

DANCY. To the life.

TWISDEN. It was mad, Captain Dancy, mad! —— But the question now is: What do you owe to your wife? She doesn't dream—I suppose?

DANCY. [*With a twitching face*] No.

TWISDEN. We can't tell what the result of this collapse will be. The police have the theft in hand. They may issue a warrant. The money could be refunded, and the costs paid—somehow that can all be managed. But it may not help. In any case, what end is served by your staying in the country? You can't save your honour—that's gone. You can't save your wife's peace of mind. If she sticks to you—do you think she will?

DANCY. Not if she's wise.

TWISDEN. Better go! There's a war in Morocco.

DANCY. [*With a bitter smile*] Good old Morocco!

TWISDEN. Will you go, then, at once, and leave me to break it to your wife?

DANCY. I don't know yet.

TWISDEN. You must decide quickly, to catch a boat train. Many a man has made good. You're a fine soldier.

DANCY. There are alternatives.

TWISDEN. Now, go straight from this office. You've a passport, I suppose; you won't need a *visa* for France, and from there you can find means to slip over. Have you got money on you? [DANCY *nods*]. We will see what we can do to stop or delay proceedings.

DANCY. It's all damned kind of you. [*With difficulty*] But I must think of my wife. Give me a few minutes.

TWISDEN. Yes, yes; go in there and think it out.

He goes to the door, Right, and opens it. DANCY *passes him and goes out.* TWISDEN *rings a bell and stands waiting.*

CLERK. [*Entering*] Yes, sir?

TWISDEN. Tell them to call a taxi.

CLERK. [*Who has a startled look*] Yes, sir. Mr

Graviter has come in, sir, with General Canynge. Are you disengaged?

TWISDEN. Yes.

The CLERK *goes out, and almost immediately* GRAVITER *and* CANYNGE *enter.*

Good-morning, General. [*To* GRAVITER] Well?

GRAVITER. Sir Frederic got up at once and said that since the publication of the numbers of those notes, information had reached him which forced him to withdraw from the case. Great sensation, of course. I left Bromley in charge. There'll be a formal verdict for the defendant, with costs. Have you told Dancy?

TWISDEN. Yes. He's in there deciding what he'll do.

CANYNGE. [*Grave and vexed*] This is a dreadful thing, Twisden. I've been afraid of it all along. A soldier! A gallant fellow, too. What on earth got into him?

TWISDEN. There's no end to human nature, General.

GRAVITER. You can see queerer things in the papers, any day.

CANYNGE. That poor young wife of his! Winsor gave me a message for you, Twisden. If money's wanted quickly to save proceedings, draw on him. Is there anything *I* can do?

TWISDEN. I've advised him to go straight off to Morocco.

CANYNGE. I don't know that an asylum isn't the place for him. He must be off his head at moments.

That jump—crazy! He'd have got a verdict on that alone—if they'd seen those balconies. I was looking at them when I was down there last Sunday. Daring thing, Twisden. Very few men, on a dark night—— He risked his life twice. That's a shrewd fellow—young De Levis. He spotted Dancy's nature.

The YOUNG CLERK *enters.*

CLERK. The taxi's here, sir. Will you see Major Colford and Miss Orme?

TWISDEN. Graviter—— No; show them in.

The YOUNG CLERK *goes.*

CANYNGE. Colford's badly cut up.

MARGARET ORME *and* COLFORD *enter.*

COLFORD. [*Striding forward*] There must be some mistake about this, Mr Twisden.

TWISDEN. Hssh! Dancy's in there. He's admitted it.

Voices are subdued at once.

COLFORD. What? [*With emotion*] If it were my own brother, I couldn't feel it more. But—damn it! What right had that fellow to chuck up the case—without letting him know, too. I came down with Dancy this morning, and he knew nothing about it.

TWISDEN. [*Coldly*] That was unfortunately unavoidable.

COLFORD. Guilty or not, you ought to have stuck to him—it's not playing the game, Mr Twisden.

TWISDEN. You must allow me to judge where my duty lay, in a very hard case.

Colford. I thought a man was safe with his solicitor.

Canynge. Colford, you don't understand professional etiquette.

Colford. No, thank God!

Twisden. When you have been as long in your profession as I have been in mine, Major Colford, you will know that duty to your calling outweighs duty to friend or client.

Colford. But I serve the Country.

Twisden. And I serve the Law, sir.

Canynge. Graviter, give me a sheet of paper. I'll write a letter for him.

Margaret. [*Going up to* Twisden] Dear Mr Jacob —pay De Levis. You know my pearls—put them up the spout again. Don't let Ronny be——

Twisden. Money isn't the point, Margaret.

Margaret. It's ghastly! It really is.

Colford. I'm going in to shake hands with him. [*He starts to cross the room*].

Twisden. Wait! We want him to go straight off to Morocco. Don't upset him. [*To* Colford *and* Margaret] I think you had better go. If, a little later, Margaret, you could go round to Mrs Dancy——

Colford. Poor little Mabel Dancy! It's perfect hell for her.

They have not seen that Dancy *has opened the door behind them.*

Dancy. It is!

They all turn round in consternation.

Colford. [*With a convulsive movement*] Old boy!

DANCY. No good, Colford. [*Gazing round at them*] Oh! clear out. I can't stand commiseration—and let me have some air.

TWISDEN *motions to* COLFORD *and* MARGARET *to go; and as he turns to* DANCY, *they go out.* GRAVITER *also moves towards the door. The* GENERAL *sits motionless.* GRAVITER *goes out.*

TWISDEN. Well?

DANCY. I'm going home, to clear up things with my wife. General Canynge, I don't quite know why I did the damned thing. But I did, and there's an end of it.

CANYNGE. Dancy, for the honour of the Army, avoid further scandal if you can. I've written a letter to a friend of mine in the Spanish War Office. It will get you a job in their war. [CANYNGE *closes the envelope*].

DANCY. Very good of you. I don't know if I can make use of it.

CANYNGE *stretches out the letter, which* TWISDEN *hands to* DANCY, *who takes it.* GRAVITER *re-opens the door.*

TWISDEN. What is it?

GRAVITER. De Levis is here.

TWISDEN. De Levis? Can't see him.

DANCY. Let him in!

After a moment's hesitation TWISDEN *nods, and* GRAVITER *goes out. The three wait in silence with their eyes fixed on the door, the* GENERAL *sitting at the table,* TWISDEN *by his chair,* DANCY *between him and the door Right.* DE LEVIS *comes in and shuts the door. He is advancing towards* TWISDEN *when his eyes fall on* DANCY, *and he stops.*

TWISDEN. You wanted to see me?

DE LEVIS. [*Moistening his lips*] Yes. I came to say that—that I overheard—I am afraid a warrant is to be issued. I wanted you to realise—it's not *my* doing. I'll give it no support. I'm content. I don't want my money. I don't even want costs. Dancy, do you understand?

DANCY *does not answer, but looks at him with nothing alive in his face but his eyes.*

TWISDEN. We are obliged to you, sir. It was good of you to come.

DE LEVIS. [*With a sort of darting pride*] Don't mistake me. I didn't come because I feel Christian; I am a Jew. I will take no money—not even that which was stolen. Give it to a charity. I'm proved right. And now I'm done with the damned thing. Good-morning!

He makes a little bow to CANYNGE *and* TWISDEN, *and turns to face* DANCY, *who has never moved. The two stand motionless, looking at each other, then* DE LEVIS *shrugs his shoulders and walks out. When he is gone there is a silence.*

CANYNGE. [*Suddenly*] You heard what he said, Dancy. You have no time to lose.

But DANCY *does not stir.*

TWISDEN. Captain Dancy?

Slowly, without turning his head, rather like a man in a dream, DANCY *walks across the room, and goes out.*

CURTAIN.

SCENE III

The DANCYS' *sitting-room, a few minutes later.*

MABEL DANCY *is sitting alone on the sofa with a newspaper on her lap; she is only just up, and has a bottle of smelling-salts in her hand. Two or three other newspapers are dumped on the arm of the sofa. She topples the one off her lap and takes up another as if she couldn't keep away from them; drops it in turn, and sits staring before her, sniffing at the salts. The door, Right, is opened and* DANCY *comes in.*

MABEL. [*Utterly surprised*] Ronny! Do they want me in Court?

DANCY. No.

MABEL. What is it, then? Why are you back?

DANCY. Spun.

MABEL. [*Blank*] Spun? What do you mean? What's spun?

DANCY. The case. They've found out through those notes.

MABEL. Oh! [*Staring at his face*] Who?

DANCY. Me!

MABEL. [*After a moment of horrified stillness*] Don't, Ronny! Oh! No! Don't! [*She buries her face in the pillows of the sofa*].

DANCY *stands looking down at her.*

DANCY. Pity you wouldn't come to Africa three months ago.

MABEL. Why didn't you tell me then? I would have gone.

DANCY. You wanted this case. Well, it's fallen down.

MABEL. Oh! Why didn't I face it? But I couldn't—I *had* to believe.

DANCY. And now you can't. It's the end, Mabel.

MABEL. [*Looking up at him*] No.

DANCY *goes suddenly on his knees and seizes her hand.*

DANCY. Forgive me!

MABEL. [*Putting her hand on his head*] Yes; oh, yes! I think I've known a long time, really. Only —why? What made you?

DANCY. [*Getting up and speaking in jerks*] It was a crazy thing to do; but, damn it, I was only looting a looter. The money was as much mine as his. A decent chap would have offered me half. You didn't see the brute look at me that night at dinner as much as to say: "You blasted fool!" It made me mad. That wasn't a bad jump—twice over. Nothing in the war took quite such nerve. [*Grimly*] I rather enjoyed that evening.

MABEL. But—money! To keep it!

DANCY. [*Sullenly*] Yes, but I had a debt to pay.

MABEL. To a woman?

DANCY. A debt of honour—it wouldn't wait.

MABEL. It was—it was to a woman. Ronny, don't lie any more.

DANCY. [*Grimly*] Well! I wanted to save your knowing. I'd promised a thousand. I had a letter from her father that morning, threatening to tell you. All the same, if that tyke hadn't jeered at me for parlour tricks!—But what's the good of all this now? [*Sullenly*] Well—it may cure you of loving me. Get over that, Mab; I never was worth it—and I'm done for!

MABEL. The woman—have you—since——?

DANCY. [*Energetically*] No! You supplanted her. But if you'd known I was leaving a woman for you, you'd never have married me. [*He walks over to the hearth*].

MABEL *too gets up. She presses her hands to her forehead, then walks blindly round to behind the sofa and stands looking straight in front of her.*

MABEL. [*Coldly*] What has happened, exactly?

DANCY. Sir Frederic chucked up the case. I've seen Twisden; they want me to run for it to Morocco.

MABEL. To the war there?

DANCY. Yes. There's to be a warrant out.

MABEL. A prosecution? Prison? Oh, go! Don't wait a minute! Go!

DANCY. Blast them!

MABEL. Oh, Ronny! Please! Please! Think what you'll want. I'll pack. Quick! No! Don't wait to take things. Have you got money?

DANCY. [*Nodding*] This'll be good-bye, then!

MABEL. [*After a moment's struggle*] Oh! No! No, no! I'll follow—I'll come out to you there.

DANCY. D'you mean you'll stick to me?

MABEL. Of course I'll stick to you.

DANCY *seizes her hand and puts it to his lips. The bell rings.*

MABEL. [*In terror*] Who's that?

The bell rings again. DANCY *moves towards the door.*

No! Let *me!*

She passes him and steals out to the outer door of the flat, where she stands listening. The bell rings again. She looks through the slit of the letter-box. While she is gone DANCY *stands quite still, till she comes back.*

MABEL. Through the letter-box—I can see—— It's—it's police. Oh! God! . . . Ronny! I can't bear it.

DANCY. Heads up, Mab! Don't show the brutes!

MABEL. Whatever happens, I'll go on loving you. If it's prison—*I'll wait.* Do you understand? I don't care what you did—I don't *care!* I'm just the same. I will be just the same when you come back to me.

DANCY. [*Slowly*] That's not in human nature.

MABEL. It is. It's in *me.*

DANCY. I've crocked up your life.

MABEL. No, no! Kiss me!

A long kiss, till the bell again startles them apart, and there is a loud knock.

DANCY. They'll break the door in. It's no good—we must open. Hold them in check a little. I want a minute or two.

MABEL. [*Clasping him*] Ronny! Oh, Ronny! It won't be for long—I'll be waiting! I'll be waiting—I swear it.

DANCY. Steady, Mab! [*Putting her back from him*] Now!

He opens the bedroom door, Left, and stands waiting for her to go. Summoning up her courage, she goes to open the outer door. A sudden change comes over DANCY'S *face; from being stony it grows almost maniacal.*

DANCY. [*Under his breath*] No! No! By God! No!

He goes out into the bedroom, closing the door behind him.

MABEL *has now opened the outer door, and disclosed* INSPECTOR DEDE *and the* YOUNG CONSTABLE *who were summoned to Meldon Court on the night of the theft, and have been witnesses in the case. Their voices are heard.*

MABEL. Yes?

INSPECTOR. Captain Dancy in, madam?

MABEL. I am not quite sure—I don't think so.

INSPECTOR. I wish to speak to him a minute. Stay here, Grover. Now, madam!

MABEL. Will you come in while I see?

She comes in, followed by the INSPECTOR.

INSPECTOR. I should think you must be sure, madam. This is not a big place.

MABEL. He was changing his clothes to go out. I think he has gone.

INSPECTOR. What's that door?

MABEL. To our bedroom.

INSPECTOR. [*Moving towards it*] He'll be in there, then.

MABEL. What do you want, Inspector?

INSPECTOR. [*Melting*] Well, madam, it's no use disguising it. I'm exceedingly sorry, but I've a warrant for his arrest.

MABEL. Inspector!

INSPECTOR. I'm sure I've every sympathy for you, madam; but I must carry out my instructions.

MABEL. And break my heart?

INSPECTOR. Well, madam, we're — we're not allowed to take that into consideration. The Law's the Law.

MABEL. Are you married?

INSPECTOR. I am.

MABEL. If you—your wife——

The INSPECTOR *raises his hand, deprecating.*

[*Speaking low*] Just half an hour! Couldn't you? It's two lives—two whole lives! We've only been married four months. Come back in half an hour. It's such a little thing—nobody will know. Nobody. Won't you?

INSPECTOR. Now, madam—you must know my duty.

MABEL. Inspector, I beseech you—just half an hour.

INSPECTOR. No, no—don't you try to undermine me—I'm sorry for you; but don't you try it! [*He tries the handle, then knocks at the door*].

DANCY'S VOICE. One minute!

INSPECTOR. It's locked. [*Sharply*] Is there another door to that room? Come, now!

The bell rings.

[*Moving towards the door, Left; to the* CONSTABLE] Who's that out there?

CONSTABLE. A lady and gentleman, sir.

INSPECTOR. What lady and—— Stand by, Grover!

DANCY'S VOICE. All right! You can come in *now.*

There is the noise of a lock being turned. And almost immediately the sound of a pistol shot in the bedroom. MABEL *rushes to the door, tears it open, and disappears within, followed by the* INSPECTOR, *just as* MARGARET ORME *and* COLFORD *come in from the passage, pursued by the* CONSTABLE. *They, too, all hurry to the bedroom door and disappear for a moment; then* COLFORD *and* MARGARET *reappear, supporting* MABEL, *who faints as they lay her on the sofa.* COLFORD *takes from her hand an envelope, and tears it open.*

COLFORD. It's addressed to *me.* [*He reads it aloud to* MARGARET *in a low voice*].

"DEAR COLFORD,—This is the only decent thing I can do. It's too damned unfair to her. It's only another jump. A pistol keeps faith. Look after her. Colford—my love to her, and you."

MARGARET *gives a sort of choking sob, then, seeing the smelling bottle, she snatches it up, and turns to revive* MABEL.

COLFORD. Leave her! The longer she's unconscious, the better.

INSPECTOR. [*Re-entering*] This is a very serious business, sir.

COLFORD. [*Sternly*] Yes, Inspector; you've done for my best friend.

INSPECTOR. I, sir? He shot himself.

COLFORD. Hari-kari.

INSPECTOR. Beg pardon?

COLFORD. [*He points with the letter to* MABEL] For her sake, and his own.

INSPECTOR. [*Putting out his hand*] I'll want that, sir.

COLFORD. [*Grimly*] You shall have it read at the inquest. Till then—it's addressed to me, and I stick to it.

INSPECTOR. Very well, sir. Do you want to have a look at him?

COLFORD *passes quickly into the bedroom, followed by the* INSPECTOR. MARGARET *remains kneeling beside* MABEL.

COLFORD *comes quickly back.* MARGARET *looks up at him. He stands very still.*

COLFORD. Neatly—through the heart.

MARGARET [*wildly*] Keeps faith! We've all done that. It's not enough.

COLFORD. [*Looking down at* MABEL] All right, old boy!

The CURTAIN *falls.*

WINDOWS

A COMEDY IN THREE ACTS
FOR IDEALISTS AND OTHERS

PERSONS OF THE PLAY

GEOFFREY MARCH . . .	Freelance in Literature
JOAN MARCH	His Wife
MARY MARCH	Their Daughter
JOHNNY MARCH	Their Son
COOK	Their Cook
MR. BLY	Their Window Cleaner
FAITH BLY	His Daughter
BLUNTER	A Strange Young Man
MR. BARNABAS	In Plain Clothes

The action passes in Geoffrey March's House, Highgate—Spring-time.

ACT I. Thursday morning. The dining-room—after breakfast.

ACT II. Thursday, a fortnight later. The dining-room—after lunch.

ACT III. The same day. The dining-room—after dinner.

ACT I

ACT I

The MARCH'S *dining-room opens through French windows on one of those gardens which seem infinite, till they are seen to be coterminous with the side walls of the house, and finite at the far end, because only the thick screen of acacias and sumachs prevents another house from being seen. The French and other windows form practically all the outer wall of that dining-room, and between them and the screen of trees lies the difference between the characters of Mr. and Mrs. March, with dots and dashes of Mary and Johnny thrown in. For instance, it has been formalised by* MRS. MARCH *but the grass has not been cut by* MR. MARCH, *and daffodils have sprung up there, which* MRS. MARCH *desires for the dining-room, but of which* MR. MARCH *says: "For God's sake, Joan, let them grow." About half therefore are now in a bowl on the breakfast table, and the other half still in the grass, in the compromise essential to lasting domesticity. A hammock under the acacias shows that* MARY *lies there sometimes with her eyes on the gleam of sunlight that comes through: and a trail in the longish grass, bordered with cigarette ends, proves that* JOHNNY *tramps there with his eyes on the ground or the stars, according. But all this is by the way, because except for a yard or two of gravel terrace outside the windows, it is all painted on the backcloth. The* MARCHES *have been at breakfast, and the round table, covered with blue linen, is thick with remains, seven baskets full. The room is gifted with old oak furniture: there is a door, stage Left, Forward; a hearth, where a fire is burning, and a high fender on which one can sit, stage Right, Middle; and in the wall below the fireplace, a service hatch covered with a sliding shutter, for the passage of dishes into the adjoining pantry. Against the wall, stage Left, is an old oak dresser, and a small writing table across the Left Back corner.* MRS. MARCH *still sits behind the coffee pot, making up her daily list on tablets with a little gold pencil fastened to her wrist. She is personable, forty-eight, trim, well-dressed, and more matter-of-fact than seems plausible.* MR. MARCH *is sitting in an armchair, sideways to the windows, smoking his pipe and reading his newspaper, with little explosions to which no one pays any attention, because it is his daily habit. He is a fine-looking man of fifty odd, with red-grey moustaches and hair, both of which stiver partly by nature and partly because his hands often push them up.* MARY *and* JOHNNY *are close to the fireplace, stage Right.* JOHNNY *sits on the fender, smoking a cigarette and warming his back. He is a commonplace-looking young man, with a decided jaw, tall, neat, soulful, who has been in the war and writes poetry.* MARY *is less ordinary; you cannot tell exactly what is the matter with her. She too is tall, a little absent, fair, and well-looking. She has a small china dog in her hand, taken from the mantelpiece, and faces the audience. As the curtain rises she is saying in her soft and pleasant voice: "Well, what is the matter with us all, Johnny?"*

JOHNNY. Stuck, as we were in the trenches—like china dogs. [*He points to the ornament in her hand.*

MR. MARCH. [*Into his newspaper*] *Damn* these people!

MARY. If there isn't an ideal left, Johnny, it's no good pretending one.

JOHNNY. That's what I'm saying: Bankrupt!

MARY. What do you want?

MRS. MARCH. [*To herself*] Mutton cutlets. Johnny, will you be in to lunch? [JOHNNY *shakes his head*] Mary? [MARY *nods*] Geof?

MR. MARCH. [*Into his paper*] Swine!

MRS. MARCH. That'll be three. [*To herself*] Spinach.

JOHNNY. If you'd just missed being killed for three blooming years for no spiritual result whatever, you'd want something to bite on, Mary.

MRS. MARCH. [*Jotting*] Soap.

JOHNNY. What price the little and weak, now? Freedom and self-determination, and all that?

MARY. Forty to one—no takers.

JOHNNY. It doesn't seem to worry *you*.

MARY. Well, what's the good?

JOHNNY. Oh, you're a looker on, Mary.

MR. MARCH. [*To his newspaper*] Of all God-forsaken time-servers!

MARY *is moved so far as to turn and look over his shoulder a minute.*

JOHNNY. Who?

MARY. Only the Old-Un.

MR. MARCH. This is absolutely Prussian!

MRS. MARCH. Soup, lobster, chicken salad. Go to Mrs. Hunt's.

MR. MARCH. And this fellow hasn't the nous to see that if ever there were a moment when it would pay us to take risks, and be generous—My hat! He ought to be—knighted! [*Resumes his paper.*

JOHNNY. [*Muttering*] You see, even Dad can't suggest chivalry without talking of payment for it. That shows how we've sunk.

MARY. [*Contemptuously*] Chivalry! Pouf! Chivalry was "off" even before the war, Johnny. Who wants chivalry?

JOHNNY. Of all shallow-pated humbug—that sneering at chivalry's the worst. Civilisation—such as we've got—is built on it.

MARY. [*Airily*] Then it's built on sand.

[*She sits beside him on the fender.*

JOHNNY. Sneering and smartness! Pah!

MARY. [*Roused*] I'll tell you what, Johnny, it's mucking about with chivalry that makes your poetry rotten. [JOHNNY *seizes her arm and twists it*] Shut up—that hurts. [JOHNNY *twists it more*] You brute! [JOHNNY *lets her arm go.*]

JOHNNY. Ha! So you don't mind taking advantage of the fact that you can cheek me with impunity, because you're weaker. You've given the whole show away, Mary. Abolish chivalry and I'll make you sit up.

MRS. MARCH. What are you two quarrelling about? Will you bring home cigarettes, Johnny—not Bogdogunov's Mamelukes—something more Anglo-American.

JOHNNY. All right! D'you want any more illustrations, Mary?

MARY. Pig!

She has risen and stands rubbing her arm and recovering her placidity, which is considerable.

MRS. MARCH. Geof, can you eat preserved peaches?

MR. MARCH. Hell! What a policy! Um?

MRS. MARCH. Can you eat preserved peaches?

MR. MARCH. Yes. [*To his paper*] Making the country stink in the eyes of the world!

MARY. Nostrils, Dad, nostrils.

[MR. MARCH *wriggles, half hearing.*

JOHNNY. [*Muttering*] Shallow idiots! Thinking we can do without chivalry!

MRS. MARCH. I'm doing my best to get a parlourmaid, to-day, Mary, but these breakfast things won't clear themselves.

MARY. I'll clear them, Mother.

MRS. MARCH. Good! [*She gets up. At the door*] Knitting silk. [*She goes out.*

JOHNNY. Mother hasn't an ounce of idealism. You might make her see stars, but never in the singular.

MR. MARCH. [*To his paper*] If God doesn't open the earth soon——

MARY. Is there anything special, Dad?

MR. MARCH. This sulphurous government. [*He drops the paper*] Give me a match, Mary.

As soon as the paper is out of his hands he becomes a different—an affable man.

MARY [*Giving him a match*] D'you mind writing in here this morning, Dad? Your study hasn't been done. There's nobody but Cook.

MR. MARCH. [*Lighting his pipe*] Anywhere.

[*He slews the armchair towards the fire.*

MARY. I'll get your things, then. [*She goes out.*

JOHNNY. [*Still on the fender*] What do you say, Dad? Is civilisation built on chivalry or on self-interest?

MR. MARCH. The question is considerable, Johnny. I should say it was built on contract, and jerry-built at that.

JOHNNY. Yes; but why do we keep contracts when we can break them with advantage and impunity?

MR. MARCH. But do we keep them?

JOHNNY. Well—say we do; otherwise you'll admit there isn't such a thing as civilisation at all. But *why* do we keep them? For instance, why don't we make Mary and Mother work for us like Kafir women? We could lick them into it. Why did we give women the vote? Why free slaves; why anything decent for the little and weak?

MR. MARCH. Well, you might say it was convenient for people living in communities.

JOHNNY. I don't think it's convenient at all. I should like to make Mary sweat. Why not jungle law, if there's nothing in chivalry.

MR. MARCH. Chivalry is altruism, Johnny. Of course it's quite a question whether altruism isn't enlightened self-interest!

JOHNNY. Oh! Damn!

The lank and shirt-sleeved figure of MR. BLY, *with a pail of water and cloths, has entered, and stands near the window, Left.*

BLY. Beg pardon, Mr. March; d'you mind me cleanin' the winders here?

MR. MARCH. Not a bit.

JOHNNY. Bankrupt of ideals. That's it!

MR. BLY *stares at him, and puts his pail down by the window.*

MARY *has entered with her father's writing materials which she puts on a stool beside him.*

MARY. Here you are, Dad! I've filled up the ink pot. Do be careful! Come on, Johnny!

She looks curiously at MR. BLY, *who has begun operations at the bottom of the left-hand window, and goes, followed by* JOHNNY.

MR. MARCH. [*Relighting his pipe and preparing his materials*] What do *you* think of things, Mr. Bly?

BLY. Not much, sir.

MR. MARCH. Ah! [*He looks up at* MR. BLY, *struck by his large philosophical eyes and moth-eaten moustache*] Nor I.

BLY. I rather thought that, sir, from your writin's.

MR. MARCH. Oh! Do you read?

BLY. I was at sea, once—formed the 'abit.

MR. MARCH. Read any of my novels?

BLY. Not to say all through—I've read some of your articles in the Sunday papers, though. Make you think!

MR. MARCH. *I'm* at sea now—don't see dry land anywhere, Mr. Bly.

BLY [*With a smile*] That's right.

MR. MARCH. D'you find that the general impression?

BLY. No. People *don't* think. You 'ave to 'ave some cause for thought.

MR. MARCH. Cause enough in the papers.

BLY. It's nearer 'ome with me. I've often thought I'd like a talk with you, sir. But I'm keepin' you.

[*He prepares to swab the pane.*

MR. MARCH. Not at all. I enjoy it. Anything to put off work.

BLY. [*Looking at* MR. MARCH, *then giving a wipe at the window*] What's drink to one is drought to another. I've seen two men take a drink out of the same can—one die of it and the other get off with a pain in his stomach.

MR. MARCH. You've seen a lot, I expect.

BLY. Ah! I've been on the beach in my day. [*He sponges at the window*] It's given me a way o' lookin' at things that I don't find in other people. Look at the 'Ome Office. *They* got no philosophy.

MR. MARCH. [*Pricking his ears*] What? Have you had dealings with them?

BLY. Over the reprieve that was got up for my daughter. But I'm keepin' you.

He swabs at the window, but always at the same pane, so that he does not advance at all.

MR. MARCH. Reprieve?

BLY. Ah! She was famous at eighteen. The *Sunday Mercury* was full of her, when she was in prison.

MR. MARCH. [*Delicately*] Dear me! I'd no idea.

BLY. She's out now; been out a fortnight. I always say that fame's ephemereal. But she'll never settle to that weavin'. Her head got turned a bit.

MR. MARCH. I'm afraid I'm in the dark, Mr. Bly.

BLY. [*Pausing—dipping his sponge in the pail and then standing with it in his hand*] Why! Don't you remember the Bly case? They sentenced 'er to be 'anged by the neck until she was dead, for smotherin' her baby. She was only eighteen at the time of speakin'.

MR. MARCH. Oh! yes! An inhuman business!

BLY. Ah! The jury recommended 'er to mercy. So they reduced it to Life.

MR. MARCH. Life! Sweet Heaven!

BLY. That's what I said; so they give her two years. I don't hold with the *Sunday Mercury*, but it put *that* over. It's a misfortune to a girl to be good-lookin'.

MR. MARCH. [*Rumpling his hair*] No, no! Dash it all! Beauty's the only thing left worth living for.

BLY. Well, I like to see green grass and a blue sky;

but it's a mistake in a 'uman bein'. Look at any young chap that's good-lookin'—'e's doomed to the screen, or hair-dressin'. Same with the girls. My girl went into an 'airdresser's at seventeen and in six months she was in trouble. When I saw 'er with a rope round her neck, as you might say, I said to meself: "Bly," I said, "you're responsible for this— If she 'adn't been good-lookin'—it'd never 'ave 'appened."

During this speech MARY *has come in with a tray, to clear the breakfast, and stands unnoticed at the dining-table, arrested by the curious words of* MR. BLY.

MR. MARCH. Your wife might not have thought that you were wholly the cause, Mr. Bly.

BLY. Ah! My wife. She's passed on. But Faith —that's my girl's name—she never was like 'er mother; there's no 'eredity in 'er on that side.

MR. MARCH. What sort of girl is she?

BLY. One for colour—likes a bit o' music—likes a dance, and a flower.

MARY. [*Interrupting softly*] Dad, I was going to clear, but I'll come back later.

MR. MARCH. Come here and listen to this! Here's a story to get your blood up! How old was the baby, Mr. Bly?

BLY. Two days—'ardly worth mentionin'. They say she 'ad the 'ighstrikes after—an' when she comes to she says: "I've saved my baby's life." An' that's true enough when you come to think what that sort o' baby goes through as a rule; dragged up by somebody else's hand, or took away by the Law. What can a workin' girl do with a baby born under the rose, as they call it? Wonderful the difference money makes when it comes to bein' outside the Law.

MR. MARCH. Right you are, Mr. Bly. God's on the side of the big battalions.

BLY. Ah! Religion! [*His eyes roll philosophically*] Did you ever read 'Aigel?

MR. MARCH. Hegel, or Haekel?

BLY. Yes; with an aitch. There's a balance abart 'im that I like. There's no doubt the Christian religion went too far. Turn the other cheek! What oh! An' this Anti-Christ, Neesha, what came in with the war —he went too far in the other direction. Neither of 'em practical men. You've got to strike a balance, and foller it.

MR. MARCH. Balance! Not much balance about us. We just run about and jump Jim Crow.

BLY. [*With a perfunctory wipe*] That's right; we 'aven't got a faith these days. But what's the use of tellin' the Englishman to act like an angel. He ain't either an angel or a blond beast. He's between the two, an 'ermumphradite. Take my daughter—— If I was a blond beast, I'd turn 'er out to starve; if I was an angel, I'd starve meself to learn her the piano. I don't do either. Why? Becos my instincts tells me not.

MR. MARCH. Yes, but my doubt is whether our instincts at this moment of the world's history are leading us up or down.

Bly. What is up and what is down? Can you answer me that? Is it up or down to get so soft that you can't take care of yourself?

Mr. March. Down.

Bly. Well, is it up or down to get so 'ard that you can't take care of others?

Mr. March. Down.

Bly. Well, there you are!

Mr. March. Then our instincts are taking us down?

Bly. Nao. They're strikin' a balance, unbeknownst, all the time.

Mr. March. You're a philosopher, Mr. Bly.

Bly. [*Modestly*] Well, I do a bit in that line, too. In my opinion Nature made the individual believe he's goin' to live after 'e's dead just to keep 'im livin' while 'e's alive—otherwise he'd 'a died out.

Mr. March. Quite a thought—quite a thought!

Bly. But I go one better than Nature. Follow your instincts is my motto.

Mr. March. Excuse me, Mr. Bly, I think Nature got hold of that before you.

Bly. [*Slightly chilled*] Well, I'm keepin' you.

Mr. March. Not at all. You're a believer in conscience, or the little voice within. When my son was very small, his mother asked him once if he didn't hear a little voice within, telling him what was right. [Mr. March *touches his diaphragm*] And he said: "I often hear little voices in here, but they never *say* anything." [Mr. Bly *cannot laugh, but he smiles*] Mary, Johnny must have been awfully like the Government.

BLY. As a matter of fact, I've got my daughter here—in obeyance.

MR. MARCH. Where? I didn't catch.

BLY. In the kitchen. Your Cook told me you couldn't get hold of an 'ouse parlour-maid. So I thought it was just a chance—you bein' broad-minded.

MR. MARCH. Oh! I see. What would your mother say, Mary?

MARY. Mother would say: "Has she had experience?"

BLY. I've told you about her experience.

MR. MARCH. Yes, but—as a parlour-maid.

BLY. Well! She can do hair. [*Observing the smile exchanged between* MR. MARCH *and* MARY] And she's quite handy with a plate.

MR. MARCH. [*Tentatively*] I'm a little afraid my wife would feel——

BLY. You see, in this weavin' shop—all the girls 'ave 'ad to be in trouble, otherwise they wouldn't take 'em. [*Apologetically towards* MARY] It's a kind of a disorderly 'ouse without the disorders. Excusin' the young lady's presence.

MARY. Oh! You needn't mind me, Mr. Bly.

MR. MARCH. And so you want her to come here? H'm!

BLY. Well I remember when she was a little bit of a thing—no higher than my knee——

[*He holds out his hand.*

MR. MARCH. [*Suddenly moved*] My God! yes. They've all been that. [*To* MARY] Where's your mother?

Mary. Gone to Mrs. Hunt's. Suppose she's engaged one, Dad?

Mr. March. Well, it's only a month's wages.

Mary. [*Softly*] She won't like it.

Mr. March. Well, let's see her, Mr. Bly; let's see her, if you don't mind.

Bly. Oh, I don't mind, sir, and she won't neither; she's used to bein' inspected by now. Why! she 'ad her bumps gone over just before she came out!

Mr. March. [*Touched on the raw again*] H'm! Too bad! Mary, go and fetch her.

[Mary, *with a doubting smile, goes out.*

[*Rising*] You might give me the details of that trial, Mr. Bly. I'll see if I can't write something that'll make people sit up. *That's* the way to send Youth to hell! How can a child who's had a rope round her neck——!

Bly. [*Who has been fumbling in his pocket, produces some yellow paper-cuttings clipped together*] Here's her references—the whole literature of the case. And here's a letter from the chaplain in one of the prisons sayin' she took a lot of interest in him; a nice young man, I believe. [*He suddenly brushes a tear out of his eye with the back of his hand*] I never thought I could 'a felt like I did over her bein' in prison. Seemed a crool senseless thing—that pretty girl o' mine. All over a baby that hadn't got used to bein' alive. Tain't as if she'd been follerin' her instincts; why, she missed that baby something crool.

Mr. March. Of course, human life—even an infant's——

BLY. I know you've got to 'ave a close time for it. But when you come to think how they take 'uman life in Injia and Ireland, and all those other places, it seems 'ard to come down like a cartload o' bricks on a bit of a girl that's been carried away by a moment's abiration.

MR. MARCH. [*Who is reading the cuttings*] H'm! What hypocrites we are!

BLY. Ah! And 'oo can tell 'oo's the father? She never give us his name. I think the better of 'er for that.

MR. MARCH. Shake hands, Mr. Bly. So do I. [BLY *wipes his hand, and* MR. MARCH *shakes it*] Loyalty's loyalty—especially when we men benefit by it.

BLY. That's right, sir.

MARY *has returned with* FAITH BLY, *who stands demure and pretty on the far side of the table, her face an embodiment of the pathetic watchful prison faculty of adapting itself to whatever may be best for its owner at the moment. At this moment it is obviously best for her to look at the ground, and yet to take in the faces of* MR. MARCH *and* MARY *without their taking her face in. A moment, for all, of considerable embarrassment.*

MR. MARCH. [*Suddenly*] Well, here we are!

The remark attracts FAITH; *she raises her eyes to his softly with a little smile, and drops them again.*

So you want to be our parlour-maid?

FAITH. Yes, please.

Mr. March. Well, Faith can remove mountains; but—er—I don't know if she can clear tables.

Bly. I've been tellin' Mr. March and the young lady what you're capable of. Show 'em what you can do with a plate.

Faith *takes the tray from the sideboard and begins to clear the table, mainly by the light of nature. After a glance,* Mr. March *looks out of the window and drums his fingers on the uncleaned pane.* Mr. Bly *goes on with his cleaning.* Mary, *after watching from the hearth, goes up and touches her father's arm.*

Mary. [*Between him and* Mr. Bly *who is bending over his bucket, softly*] You're not watching, Dad.

Mr. March. It's too pointed.

Mary. We've got to satisfy mother.

Mr. March. I can satisfy her better if I don't look.

Mary. You're right.

Faith *has paused a moment and is watching them. As* Mary *turns, she resumes her operations.* Mary *joins, and helps her finish clearing, while the two men converse.*

Bly. Fine weather, sir, for the time of year.

Mr. March. It is. The trees are growing.

Bly. Ah! I wouldn't be surprised to see a change of Government before long. I've seen 'uge trees in Brazil without any roots—seen 'em come down with a crash.

Mr. March. Good image, Mr. Bly. Hope you're right!

BLY. Well, Governments! They're all the same—Butter when they're out of power, and blood when they're in. And Lord! 'ow they do abuse other Governments for doin' the things they do themselves. Excuse me, I'll want her dosseer back, sir, when you're done with it.

MR. MARCH. Yes, yes. [*He turns, rubbing his hands at the cleared table*] Well, that seems all right! And you can do hair?

FAITH. Oh! Yes, I can do hair.

Again that little soft look, and smile so carefully adjusted.

MR. MARCH. That's important, don't you think, Mary? [MARY, *accustomed to candour, smiles dubiously.*] [*Brightly*] Ah! And cleaning plate? What about that?

FAITH. Of course, if I had the opportunity——

MARY. You haven't—so far?

FAITH. Only tin things.

MR. MARCH. [*Feeling a certain awkwardness*] Well, I daresay we can find some for you. Can you—er—be firm on the telephone?

FAITH. Tell them you're engaged when you're not? Oh! yes.

MR. MARCH. Excellent! Let's see, Mary, what else is there?

MARY. Waiting, and house work.

MR. MARCH. Exactly.

FAITH. I'm very quick. I—I'd like to come. [*She looks down*] I don't care for what I'm doing now. It makes you feel your position.

MARY. Aren't they nice to you?

FAITH. Oh! yes—kind; but— [*She looks up*] it's against my instincts.

MR. MARCH. Oh! [*Quizzically*] You've got a disciple, Mr. Bly.

BLY. [*Rolling his eyes at his daughter*] Ah! but you mustn't 'ave instincts here, you know. You've got a chance, and you must come to stay, and do yourself credit.

FAITH. [*Adapting her face*] Yes, I know, I'm very lucky.

MR. MARCH. [*Deprecating thanks and moral precept*] That's all right! Only, Mr. Bly, I can't absolutely answer for Mrs. March. She may think——

MARY. There *is* Mother; I heard the door.

BLY. [*Taking up his pail*] I quite understand, sir; I've been a married man myself. It's very queer the way women look at things. I'll take her away now, and come back presently and do these other winders. You can talk it over by yourselves. But if you do see your way, sir, I shan't forget it in an 'urry. To 'ave the responsibility of her—really, it's dreadful.

FAITH'S *face has grown sullen during this speech, but it clears up in another little soft look at* MR. MARCH, *as she and* MR. BLY *go out.*

MR. MARCH. Well, Mary, have I done it?

MARY. You have, Dad.

MR. MARCH. [*Running his hands through his hair*] Pathetic little figure! Such infernal inhumanity!

MARY. How are you going to put it to mother?

MR. MARCH. Tell her the story, and pitch it strong.

MARY. Mother's not impulsive.

MR. MARCH. We *must* tell her, or she'll think me mad.

MARY. She'll do that, anyway, dear.

MR. MARCH. Here she is! Stand by!

He runs his arm through MARY'S, *and they sit on the fender, at bay.* MRS. MARCH *enters, Left.*

MR. MARCH. Well, what luck?

MRS. MARCH. None.

MR. MARCH. [*Unguardedly*] Good!

MRS. MARCH. What?

MR. MARCH. [*Cheerfully*] Well, the fact is, Mary and I have caught one for you; Mr. Bly's daughter——

MRS. MARCH. Are you out of your senses? Don't you know that she's the girl who——

MR. MARCH. That's it. She wants a lift.

MRS. MARCH. Geof!

MR. MARCH. Well, don't we want a maid?

MRS. MARCH. [*Ineffably*] Ridiculous!

MR. MARCH. We tested her, didn't we, Mary?

MRS. MARCH. [*Crossing to the bell, and ringing*] You'll just send for Mr. Bly and get rid of her again.

MR. MARCH. Joan, if we comfortable people can't put ourselves a little out of the way to give a helping hand——

MRS. MARCH. To girls who smother their babies?

MR. MARCH. Joan, I revolt. I won't be a hypocrite and a Pharisee.

MRS. MARCH. Well, for goodness sake let *me* be one.

MARY. [*As the door opens*] Here's Cook!

COOK *stands—sixty, stout, and comfortable—with a crumpled smile.*

COOK. Did you ring, ma'am?

MR. MARCH. We're in a moral difficulty, Cook, so naturally we come to you.

[COOK *beams.*

MRS. MARCH. [*Impatiently*] Nothing of the sort, Cook; it's a question of common sense.

COOK. Yes, ma'am.

MRS MARCH. That girl, Faith Bly, wants to come here as parlour-maid. Absurd!

MR MARCH. You know her story, Cook? I want to give the poor girl a chance. Mrs. March thinks it's *taking* chances. What do you say?

COOK. Of course, it is a risk, sir; but there! you've got to take 'em to get maids nowadays. If it isn't in the past, it's in the future. I daresay I could learn 'er.

MRS. MARCH. It's not her work, Cook, it's her instincts. A girl who smothered a baby that she oughtn't to have had——

MR. MARCH. [*Remonstrant*] If she hadn't had it how could she have smothered it?

COOK. [*Soothingly*] Perhaps she's repented, ma'am.

MRS. MARCH. Of course she's repented. But did you ever know repentance change anybody, Cook?

COOK. [*Smiling*] Well, generally it's a way of gettin' ready for the next.

MRS. MARCH. Exactly.

MR. MARCH. If we never get another chance *because* we repent——

COOK. I always think of Master Johnny, ma'am, and my jam; he used to repent so beautiful, dear little feller—such a conscience! I never could bear to lock it away.

MRS. MARCH. Cook, you're wandering. I'm surprised at your encouraging the idea; I really am.

[COOK *plaits her hands.*

MR. MARCH. Cook's been in the family longer than I have—haven't you, Cook? [COOK *beams*] She knows much more about a girl like that than we do.

COOK. We had a girl like her, I remember, in your dear mother's time, Mr. Geoffrey.

MR. MARCH. How did she turn out?

COOK. Oh! She didn't.

MRS. MARCH. There!

MR. MARCH. Well, I can't bear behaving like everybody else. Don't you think we might give her a chance, Cook?

COOK. My 'eart says yes, ma'am.

MR. MARCH. Ha!

COOK. And my 'ead says no, sir.

MRS. MARCH. Yes!

MR. MARCH. Strike your balance, Cook.

COOK *involuntarily draws her joined hands sharply in upon her amplitude.*

Well? . . . I didn't catch the little voice within.

COOK. Ask Master Johnny, sir; he's been in the war.

MR. MARCH. [*To* MARY] Get Johnny.

[MARY *goes out*.

MRS. MARCH. What on earth has the war to do with it?

COOK. The things he tells me, ma'am, is too wonderful for words. He's 'ad to do with prisoners and generals, every sort of 'orror.

MR. MARCH. Cook's quite right. The war destroyed all our ideals and probably created the baby.

MRS. MARCH. It didn't smother it; or condemn the girl.

MR. MARCH. [*Running his hands through his hair*] The more I think of that——! [*He turns away*.

MRS. MARCH. [*Indicating her husband*] You see, Cook, that's the mood in which I have to engage a parlour-maid. What am I to do with your master?

COOK. It's an 'ealthy rage, ma'am.

MRS. MARCH. I'm tired of being the only sober person in this house.

COOK. [*Reproachfully*] Oh! ma'am, I never touch a drop.

MRS. MARCH. I didn't mean anything of that sort. But they do break out so.

COOK. Not Master Johnny.

MRS. MARCH. Johnny! He's the worst of all. His poetry is nothing but one long explosion.

MR. MARCH. [*Coming from the window*] I say: We ought to have faith and jump.

MRS. MARCH. If we do have Faith, we shall jump.

COOK. [*Blankly*] Of course, in the Bible they 'ad faith, and just look what it did to them!

MR. MARCH. I mean faith in human instincts, human nature, Cook.

COOK. [*Scandalised*] Oh! no, sir, *not* human nature; I never let that get the upper hand.

MR. MARCH. You talk to Mr. Bly. He's a remarkable man.

COOK. I do, sir, every fortnight when he does the kitchen windows.

MR. MARCH. Well, doesn't he impress you?

COOK. Ah! When he's got a drop o' stout in 'im—Oh! dear! [*She smiles placidly.*]

[JOHNNY *has come in*]

MR. MARCH. Well, Johnny, has Mary told you?

MRS. MARCH. [*Looking at his face*] Now, my dear boy, don't be hasty and foolish!

JOHNNY. Of course you ought to take her, Mother.

MRS. MARCH. [*Fixing him*] Have you seen her, Johnny?

JOHNNY. She's in the hall, poor little devil, waiting for her sentence.

MRS. MARCH. There are plenty of other chances, Johnny. Why on earth should we——?

JOHNNY. Mother, it's just an instance. When something comes along that takes a bit of doing—Give it to the other chap!

MR. MARCH. Bravo, Johnny!

MRS. MARCH. [*Drily*] Let me see, which of us will have to put up with her shortcomings—Johnny or I?

MARY. She looks quick, Mother.

MRS. MARCH. Girls pick up all sorts of things in

prison. We can hardly expect her to be honest. You don't mind that, I suppose?

JOHNNY. It's a chance to make something decent out of her.

MRS. MARCH. I can't understand this passion for vicarious heroism, Johnny.

JOHNNY. Vicarious!

MRS. MARCH. Well, where do you come in? You'll make poems about the injustice of the Law. Your father will use her in a novel. She'll wear Mary's blouses, and everybody will be happy—except Cook and me.

MR. MARCH. Hang it all, Joan, you might be the Great Public itself!

MRS. MARCH. I am—get all the kicks and none of the ha'pence.

JOHNNY. We'll all help you.

MRS. MARCH. For Heaven's sake—no, Johnny!

MR. MARCH. Well, make up your mind!

MRS. MARCH. It was made up long ago.

JOHNNY. [*Gloomily*] The more I see of things the more disgusting they seem. I don't see what we're living for. All right. Chuck the girl out, and let's go rooting along with our noses in the dirt.

MR. MARCH. Steady, Johnny!

JOHNNY. Well, Dad, there was one thing anyway we learned out there— When a chap was in a hole—to pull him out, even at a risk.

MRS. MARCH. There are people who—the moment you pull them out—jump in again.

MARY. We can't tell till we've tried, Mother.

COOK. It's wonderful the difference good food'll make, ma'am.

MRS. MARCH. Well, you're all against me. Have it your own way, and when you regret it—remember me!

MR. MARCH. We will—we will! That's settled, then. Bring her in and tell her. We'll go on to the terrace.

He goes out through the window, followed by JOHNNY.

MARY. [*Opening the door*] Come in, please.

FAITH *enters and stands beside* COOK, *close to the door.* MARY *goes out.*

MRS. MARCH. [*Matter of fact in defeat as in victory*] You want to come to us, I hear.

FAITH. Yes.

MRS. MARCH. And you don't know much?

FAITH. No.

COOK [*Softly*] Say ma'am, dearie.

MRS. MARCH. Cook is going to do her best for you. Are you going to do yours for us?

FAITH. [*With a quick look up*] Yes—ma'am.

MRS. MARCH. Can you begin at once?

FAITH. Yes.

MRS. MARCH. Well, then, Cook will show you where things are kept, and how to lay the table and that. Your wages will be thirty until we see where we are. Every other Sunday, and Thursday afternoon. What about dresses?

FAITH. [*Looking at her dress*] I've only got this—I had it before, of course, it hasn't been worn.

MRS. MARCH. Very neat. But I meant for the house. You've no money, I suppose?

FAITH. Only one pound thirteen, ma'am.

MRS. MARCH. We shall have to find you some dresses, then. Cook will take you to-morrow to Needham's. You needn't wear a cap unless you like. Well, I hope you'll get on. I'll leave you with Cook now.

After one look at the girl, who is standing motionless, she goes out.

FAITH. [*With a jerk, as if coming out of plaster of Paris*] *She's* never been in prison!

COOK. [*Comfortably*] Well, my dear, we can't all of us go everywhere, 'owever 'ard we try!

She is standing back to the dresser, and turns to it, opening the right-hand drawer.

COOK. Now, 'ere's the wine. The master likes 'is glass. And 'ere's the spirits in the tantaliser—'tisn't ever kept locked, in case Master Johnny should bring a friend in. Have you noticed Master Johnny? [FAITH *nods*] Ah! He's a dear boy; and wonderful high-principled since he's been in the war. He'll come to me sometimes and say: "Cook, we're all going to the devil!" They think 'ighly of 'im as a poet. He spoke up for you beautiful.

FAITH. Oh! He spoke up for me?

COOK. Well, of course they had to talk you over.

FAITH. I wonder if they think I've got feelings.

COOK. [*Regarding her moody, pretty face*] Why! We all have feelin's!

FAITH. Not below three hundred a year.

COOK. [*Scandalised*] Dear, dear! Where were you educated?

FAITH. I wasn't.

COOK. Tt! Well—it's wonderful what a change there is in girls since my young days [*Pulling out a drawer*] Here's the napkins. You change the master's every day at least because of his moustache; and the others every two days, but always clean ones Sundays. Did you keep Sundays in *there?*

FAITH. [*Smiling*] Yes. Longer chapel.

COOK. It'll be a nice change for you, here. They don't go to Church; they're agnosticals. [*Patting her shoulder*] How old are you?

FAITH. Twenty.

COOK. Think of that—and such a life! Now, dearie, I'm your friend. Let the present bury the past—as the sayin' is. Forget all about yourself, and you'll be a different girl in no time.

FAITH. Do you want to be a different woman?

COOK *is taken flat aback by so sudden a revelation of the pharisaism of which she has not been conscious.*

COOK. Well! You *are* sharp! [*Opening another dresser drawer*] Here's the vinegar! And here's the sweets, and [*rather anxiously*] you mustn't eat them.

FAITH. I wasn't in for theft.

COOK. [*Shocked at such rudimentary exposure of her natural misgivings*] No, no! But girls have appetites.

FAITH. *They* didn't get much chance where I've been.

Cook. Ah! You must tell me all about it. Did you have adventures?

Faith. There isn't such a thing in a prison.

Cook. You don't say! Why, in the books they're escapin' all the time. But books is books; I've always said so. How were the men?

Faith. Never saw a man—only a chaplain.

Cook. Dear, dear! They must be quite fresh to you, then! How long was it?

Faith. Two years.

Cook. And never a day out? What did you do all the time? Did they learn you anything?

Faith. Weaving. That's why I hate it.

Cook. Tell me about your poor little baby. I'm sure you meant it for the best.

Faith. [*Sardonically*] Yes; I was afraid they'd make it a ward in Chancery.

Cook. Oh! dear—what things do come into your head! Why! No one can take a baby from its mother.

Faith. Except the Law.

Cook. Tt! Tt! Well! Here's the pickled onions. Miss Mary loves 'em! Now then, let me see you lay the cloth.

She takes a tablecloth out, hands it to Faith, *and while the girl begins to unfold the cloth she crosses to the service shutter.*

And here's where we pass the dishes through into the pantry.

The door is opened, and Mrs. March's *voice says:* "Cook—a minute!"

[*Preparing to go*] Salt cellars one at each corner—four,

and the peppers. [*From the door*] Now the decanters. Oh! you'll soon get on. [MRS. MARCH: "Cook!"] Yes, ma'am. [*She goes.*

FAITH, *left alone, stands motionless, biting her pretty lip, her eyes mutinous. Hearing footsteps, she looks up.* MR. BLY, *with his pail and cloths, appears outside.*

BLY. [*Preparing to work, while* FAITH *prepares to set the salt cellars*] So you've got it! You never know your luck. Up to-day and down to-morrow. I'll 'ave a glass over this to-night. What d'you get?

FAITH. Thirty.

BLY. It's not the market price, still, you're not the market article. Now, put a good heart into it and get to know your job; you'll find Cook full o' philosophy if you treat her right—she can make a dumplin' with anybody. But look 'ere; you confine yourself to the ladies!

FAITH. I don't want your advice, father.

BLY. I know parents are out of date; still, I've put up with a lot on your account, so gimme a bit of me own back.

FAITH. I don't know whether I shall like this. I've been shut up so long. I want to see some life.

BLY. Well, that's natural. But I want you to do well. I suppose you'll be comin' 'ome to fetch your things to-night?

FAITH. Yes.

BLY. I'll have a flower for you. What'd you like—daffydils?

FAITH. No; one with a scent to it.

BLY. I'll ask at Mrs. Bean's round the corner. She'll pick 'em out from what's over. Never 'ad much nose for a flower meself. I often thought you'd like a flower when you was in prison.

FAITH. [*A little touched*] Did you? Did you—really?

BLY. Ah! I suppose I've drunk more glasses over your bein' in there than over anything that ever 'appened to me. Why! I couldn't relish the war for it! And I suppose you 'ad none to relish. Well, it's over. So, put an 'eart into it.

FAITH. I'll try.

BLY. "There's compensation for everything"—'Aigel says. At least, if it wasn't 'Aigel it was one o' the others. I'll move on to the study now. Ah! He's got some winders there lookin' right over the country. And a wonderful lot o' books, if you feel inclined for a read one of these days.

COOK'S VOICE. Faith!

> FAITH *sets down the salt cellar in her hand, puts her tongue out a very little, and goes out into the hall.* MR. BLY *is gathering up his pail and cloths when* MR. MARCH *enters at the window.*

MR. MARCH. So it's fixed up, Mr. Bly.

BLY. [*Raising himself*] I'd like to shake your 'and, sir. [*They shake hands*] It's a great weight off my mind.

MR. MARCH. It's rather a weight on my wife's, I'm afraid. But we must hope for the best. The country wants rain, but—I doubt if we shall get it with this Government.

BLY. Ah! We want the good old times—when you could depend on the seasons. The further you look back the more dependable the times get; 'ave you noticed that, sir?

MR. MARCH. [*Suddenly*] Suppose they'd hanged your daughter, Mr. Bly. What would you have done?

BLY. Well, to be quite frank, I should 'ave got drunk on it.

MR. MARCH. Public opinion's always in advance of the Law. I think your daughter's a most pathetic little figure.

BLY. Her looks *are* against her. I never found a man that didn't.

MR. MARCH. [*A little disconcerted*] Well, we'll try and give her a good show here.

BLY. [*Taking up his pail*] I'm greatly obliged; she'll appreciate anything you can do for her. [*He moves to the door and pauses there to say*] Fact is—her winders wants cleanin', she 'ad a dusty time in there.

MR. MARCH. I'm sure she had.

MR. BLY *passes out, and* MR. MARCH *busies himself in gathering up his writing things preparatory to seeking his study. While he is so engaged* FAITH *comes in. Glancing at him, she resumes her placing of the decanters, as* JOHNNY *enters by the window, and comes down to his father by the hearth.*

JOHNNY. [*Privately*] If you haven't begun your morning, Dad, you might just tell me what you think of these verses.

He puts a sheet of notepaper before his father, who takes it and begins to con over the verses thereon, while JOHNNY *looks carefully at his nails.*

MR. MARCH. Er—I—I like the last line awfully, Johnny.

JOHNNY. [*Gloomily*] What about the other eleven?

MR. MARCH. [*Tentatively*] Well—old man, I—er—think perhaps it'd be stronger if they were out.

JOHNNY. Good God!

He takes back the sheet of paper, clutches his brow, and crosses to the door. As he passes FAITH, *she looks up at him with eyes full of expression.* JOHNNY *catches the look, jibs ever so little, and goes out.*

COOK'S VOICE. [*Through the door, which is still ajar*] Faith!

FAITH *puts the decanters on the table, and goes quickly out.*

MR. MARCH. [*Who has seen this little by-play—to himself—in a voice of dismay*] Oh! oh! I wonder!

CURTAIN.

ACT II

ACT II

A fortnight later in the MARCH's *dining-room; a day of violent April showers. Lunch is over and the table littered with remains—twelve baskets full.*

MR. MARCH *and* MARY *have lingered.* MR. MARCH *is standing by the hearth where a fire is burning, filling a fountain pen.* MARY *sits at the table opposite, pecking at a walnut.*

MR. MARCH. [*Examining his fingers*] What it is to have an inky present! Suffer with me, Mary!

MARY. "Weep ye no more, sad Fountains!
Why need ye flow so fast?"

MR. MARCH. [*Pocketing his pen*] Coming with me to the British Museum? I want to have a look at the Assyrian reliefs.

MARY. Dad, have you noticed Johnny?

MR. MARCH. I have.

MARY. Then only Mother hasn't.

MR. MARCH. I've always found your mother extremely good at seeming not to notice things, Mary.

MARY. Faith! She's got on very fast this fortnight.

MR. MARCH. The glad eye, Mary. I got it that first morning.

MARY. *You,* Dad?

MR. MARCH. No, no! Johnny got it, and I got him getting it.

MARY. What are you going to do about it?

MR. MARCH. What *does* one do with a glad eye that belongs to some one else?

MARY. [*Laughing*] No. But, seriously, Dad, Johnny's not like you and me. Why not speak to Mr. Bly?

MR. MARCH. Mr. Bly's eyes are not glad.

MARY. Dad! Do be serious! Johnny's capable of anything except a sense of humour.

MR. MARCH. The girl's past makes it impossible to say anything to her.

MARY. Well, I warn you. Johnny's very queer just now; he's in the "lose the world to save your soul" mood. It really is *too* bad of that girl. After all, we did what most people wouldn't.

MR. MARCH. Come! Get your hat on, Mary, or we shan't make the Tube before the next shower.

MARY. [*Going to the door*] Something must be done.

MR. MARCH. As you say, something—— Ah! Mr. Bly!

MR. BLY, *in precisely the same case as a fortnight ago, with his pail and cloths, is coming in.*

BLY. Afternoon, sir! Shall I be disturbing you if I do the winders here?

MR. MARCH. Not at all.

[MR. BLY *crosses to the windows.*

MARY. [*Pointing to* MR. BLY'S *back*] Try!

BLY. Showery, sir.

MR. MARCH. Ah!

BLY. Very tryin' for winders. [*Resting*] My daughter givin' satisfaction, I hope?

MR. MARCH. [*With difficulty*] Er—in her work, I believe, coming on well. But the question is, Mr. Bly, do—er—any of us ever really give satisfaction except to ourselves?

BLY. [*Taking it as an invitation to his philosophical vein*] Ah! that's one as goes to the roots of 'uman nature. There's a lot of disposition in all of us. And what I always say is: One man's disposition is another man's indisposition.

MR. MARCH. By George! Just hits the mark.

BLY. [*Filling his sponge*] Question is: How far are you to give rein to your disposition? When I was in Durban, Natal, I knew a man who had the biggest disposition I ever come across. 'E struck 'is wife, 'e smoked opium, 'e was a liar, 'e gave all the rein 'e could, and yet withal one of the pleasantest men I ever met.

MR. MARCH. Perhaps in giving rein he didn't strike you.

BLY. [*With a big wipe, following his thought*] He said to me once: "Joe," he said, "if I was to hold meself in, I should be a devil." There's where you get it. Policemen, priests, prisoners. Cab'net Ministers, any one who leads an unnatural life, see how it twists 'em. You can't suppress a thing without it swellin' you up in another place.

MR. MARCH. And the moral of that is——?

BLY. Follow your instincts. You see—if I'm not keepin' you—now that we ain't got no faith, as we were sayin' the other day, no Ten Commandments in black an' white—we've just got to be 'uman bein's—raisin' Cain, and havin' feelin' hearts. What's the use of all these lofty ideas that you can't live up to? Liberty, Fraternity, Equality, Democracy—see what comes o' fightin' for 'em! 'Ere we are—wipin' out the lot. We thought they was fixed stars; they was only comets—hot air. No; trust 'uman nature, I say, and follow your instincts.

MR. MARCH. We were talking of your daughter—I—I——

BLY. There's a case in point. Her instincts was starved goin' on for three years, because, mind you, they kept her hangin' about in prison months before they tried her. I read your article, and I thought to meself after I'd finished: Which would I feel smallest—if I was—the Judge, the Jury, or the 'Ome Secretary? It *was* a treat, that article! They ought to abolish that in'uman "To be hanged by the neck until she is dead." It's my belief they only keep it because it's [illegible], that and the wigs—they're hard up for a [illegible] beauty in the Courts of Law. Excuse my 'and, sir; I do thank you for that article.

He extends his wiped hand, which MR. MARCH *shakes with the feeling that he is always shaking* MR. BLY'S *hand.*

MR. MARCH. But, *àpropos* of your daughter, Mr. Bly. I suppose none of us ever change our natures.

Bly. [*Again responding to the appeal that he senses to his philosophical vein*] Ah! but 'oo can see what our natures are? Why, I've known people that could see nothin' but theirselves and their own families, unless they was drunk. At my daughter's trial, I see right into the lawyers, judge and all. There she was, hub of the whole thing, and all they could see of her was 'ow far she affected 'em personally—one tryin' to get 'er guilty, the other tryin' to get 'er off, and the judge summin' 'er up cold-blooded.

Mr. March. But that's what they're paid for, Mr. Bly.

Bly. Ah! But which of 'em was thinkin': "'Ere's a little bit o' warm life on its own. 'Ere's a little dancin' creature. What's she feelin', wot's 'er complaint?" —impersonal-like. I like to see a man do a bit of speculatin', with his mind off of 'imself, for once.

Mr. March. "The man that hath not speculation in his soul."

Bly. That's right, sir. When I see a mangy cat or a dog that's lost, or a fellow-creature down on his luck, I always try to put meself in his place. It's a weakness I've got.

Mr. March. [*Warmly*] A deuced good one. Shake——

He checks himself, but Mr. Bly *has wiped his hand and extended it.*

While the shake is in progress Mary *returns, and, having seen it to a safe conclusion, speaks.*

Mary. Coming, Dad?

Mr. March. Excuse me, Mr. Bly, I must away.

He goes towards the door, and Bly *dips his sponge.*

Mary. [*In a low voice*] Well?

Mr. March. Mr. Bly is like all the greater men I know—he can't listen.

Mary. But you were shaking——

Mr. March. Yes; it's a weakness we have—every three minutes.

Mary. [*Bubbling*] Dad—silly!

Mr. March. Very!

As they go out Mr. Bly *pauses in his labours to catch, as it were, a philosophical reflection. He resumes the wiping of a pane, while quietly, behind him,* Faith *comes in with a tray. She is dressed now in lilac-coloured linen, without a cap, and looks prettier than ever. She puts the tray down on the sideboard with a clap that attracts her father's attention, and stands contemplating the debris on the table.*

Bly. Winders! There they are! Clean, dirty! All sorts—All round yer! Winders!

Faith. [*With disgust*] Food!

Bly. Ah! Food and winders! That's life!

Faith. Eight times a day—four times for them and four times for us. I hate food!

[*She puts a chocolate into her mouth.*

Bly. 'Ave some philosophy. I might just as well hate me winders.

Faith. Well! [*She begins to clear.*

Bly. [*Regarding her*] Look 'ere, my girl! Don't you

forget that there ain't many winders in London out o' which they look as philosophical as these here. Beggars can't be choosers.

FAITH. [*Sullenly*] Oh! Don't go on at me!

BLY. They spoiled your disposition in that place, I'm afraid.

FAITH. Try it, and see what they do with yours.

BLY. Well, I may come to it yet.

FAITH. You'll get no windows to look out of there; a little bit of a thing with bars to it, and lucky if it's not thick glass. [*Standing still and gazing past* MR. BLY] No sun, no trees, no faces—people don't pass in the sky, not even angels.

BLY. Ah! But you shouldn't brood over it. I knew a man in Valpiraso that 'ad spent 'arf 'is life in prison—a *jolly* feller; I forget what 'e'd done, somethin' bloody. I want to see you like him. Aren't you happy here?

FAITH. It's right enough, so long as I get out.

BLY. This Mr. March—he's like all these novel-writers—thinks 'e knows 'uman nature, but of course 'e don't. Still, I can talk to 'im—got an open mind, and hates the Gover'ment. That's the two great things. Mrs. March, so far as I see, 'as got her head screwed on much tighter.

FAITH. She has.

BLY. What's the young man like? He's a long feller.

FAITH. Johnny? [*With a shrug and a little smile*] Johnny.

BLY. Well, that gives a very good idea of him. They say 'e's a poet; does 'e leave 'em about?

FAITH. I've seen one or two.

BLY. What's their tone?

FAITH. All about the condition of the world; and the moon.

BLY. Ah! Depressin'. And the young lady?

[FAITH *shrugs her shoulders.*

Um—'ts what I thought. *She* 'asn't moved much with the times. She thinks she 'as, but she 'asn't. Well, they seem a pleasant family. Leave you to yourself. 'Ow's Cook?

FAITH. Not much company.

BLY. More body than mind? Still, you get out, don't you?

FAITH. [*With a slow smile*] Yes. [*She gives a sudden little twirl, and puts her hands up to her hair before the mirror*] My afternoon to-day. It's fine in the streets, after—being in *there.*

BLY. Well! Don't follow your instincts too much, that's all! I must get on to the drawin'-room now. There's a shower comin'. [*Philosophically*] It's 'ardly worth while to do these winders. You clean 'em, and they're dirty again in no time. It's like life. And people talk o' progress. What a sooperstition! Of course there ain't progress; it's a world-without-end affair. You've got to make up your mind to it, and not be discouraged. All this depression comes from 'avin' 'igh 'opes. 'Ave low 'opes, and you'll be all right.

He takes up his pail and cloths and moves out through the windows.

FAITH *puts another chocolate into her mouth, and taking up a flower, twirls round with it held to her nose, and looks at herself in the glass over the hearth. She is still looking at herself when she sees in the mirror a reflection of* JOHNNY, *who has come in. Her face grows just a little scared, as if she had caught the eye of a warder peering through the peep-hole of her cell door, then brazens, and slowly sweetens as she turns round to him.*

JOHNNY. Sorry! [*He has a pipe in his hand and wears a Norfolk jacket*] Fond of flowers?

FAITH. Yes. [*She puts back the flower*] Ever so!

JOHNNY. Stick to it. Put it in your hair; it'll look jolly. How do you like it here?

FAITH. It's quiet.

JOHNNY. Ha! I wonder if you've got the feeling I have. We've both had hell, you know; I had three years of it out there, and you've had three years of it here. The feeling that you can't catch up; can't live fast enough to get even.

[FAITH *nods.*

Nothing's big enough; nothing's worth while enough—is it?

FAITH. I don't know. I know I'd like to bite.

[*She draws her lips back.*

JOHNNY. Ah! Tell me all about your beastly time; it'll do you good. You and I are different from anybody else in this house. We've lived—they've just vegetated. Come on; tell me!

FAITH, *who up to now has looked on him as a young male, stares at him for the first time without sex in her eyes.*

FAITH. I can't. We didn't talk in there, you know.

JOHNNY. Were you fond of the chap who——?

FAITH. No. Yes. I suppose I was—once.

JOHNNY. He must have been rather a swine.

FAITH. He's dead.

JOHNNY. Sorry! Oh, sorry!

FAITH. I've forgotten all that.

JOHNNY. Beastly things, babies; and absolutely unnecessary in the present state of the world.

FAITH. [*With a faint smile*] My baby wasn't beastly; but I—I got upset.

JOHNNY. Well, I should think so!

FAITH. My friend in the manicure came and told me about hers when I was lying in the hospital. She couldn't have it with her, so it got neglected and died.

JOHNNY. Um! I believe that's quite common.

FAITH. And she told me about another girl—the Law took her baby from her. And after she was gone, I—got all worked up—— [*She hesitates, then goes swiftly on*] And I looked at mine; it was asleep just here, quite close. I just put out my arm like that, over its face—*quite* soft—I didn't hurt it. I didn't really. [*She suddenly swallows, and her lips quiver*] I didn't feel anything under my arm. And—and a beast of a nurse came on me, and said: "You've smothered your baby, you wretched girl!" I didn't want to kill it—I only wanted to save it from living. And when I looked at it, I went off screaming.

JOHNNY. I nearly screamed when I saved my first German from living. I never felt the same again. They say the human race has got to go on, but I say they've first got to prove that the human race wants to. Would you rather be alive or dead?

FAITH. Alive.

JOHNNY. But would you have in prison?

FAITH. I don't know. You can't tell anything in there. [*With sudden vehemence*] I wish I had my baby back, though. It was mine; and I—I don't like thinking about it.

JOHNNY. I know. I hate to think about anything I've killed, really. At least, I should—but it's better not to think.

FAITH. I could have killed that judge.

JOHNNY. Did he come the heavy father? That's what I can't stand. When they jaw a chap and hang him afterwards. Or was he one of the joking ones?

FAITH. I've sat in my cell and cried all night—night after night, I have. [*With a little laugh*] I cried all the softness out of me.

JOHNNY. You never believed they were going to hang you, did you?

FAITH. I didn't care if they did—not then.

JOHNNY. [*With a reflective grunt*] You had a much worse time than I. You were lonely——

FAITH. Have you been in a prison, ever?

JOHNNY. No, thank God!

FAITH. It's awfully clean.

JOHNNY. You bet.

FAITH. And it's stone cold. It turns your heart.

JOHNNY. Ah! Did you ever see a stalactite?

FAITH. What's that?

JOHNNY. In caves. The water drops like tears, and each drop has some sort of salt, and leaves it behind till there's just a long salt petrified drip hanging from the roof.

FAITH. Ah! [*Staring at him*] I used to stand behind my door. I'd stand there sometimes I don't know how long. I'd listen and listen—the noises are all hollow in a prison. You'd think you'd get used to being shut up, but I never did.

[JOHNNY *utters a deep grunt.*

It's awful the feeling you get here—so tight and chokey. People who are free don't know what it's like to be shut up. If I'd had a proper window even—— When you can see things living, it makes you feel alive.

JOHNNY. [*Catching her arm*] *We*'ll make you feel alive again.

FAITH *stares at him; sex comes back to her eyes. She looks down.*

I bet you used to enjoy life, before.

FAITH. [*Clasping her hands*] Oh! yes, I did. And I love getting out now. I've got a fr—— [*She checks herself*] The streets are beautiful, aren't they? Do you know Orleens Street?

JOHNNY. [*Doubtful*] No-o. . . . Where?

FAITH. At the corner out of the Regent. That's where we had our shop. I like the hair-dressing. We had fun. Perhaps I've seen you before. Did you ever come in there?

JOHNNY. No.

FAITH. I'd go back there; only they wouldn't take me—I'm too conspicuous now.

JOHNNY. I expect you're well out of that.

FAITH. [*With a sigh*] But I did like it. I felt free. We had an hour off in the middle of the day; you could go where you liked; and then, after hours—I love the streets at night—all lighted. Olga—that's one of the other girls—and I used to walk about for hours. That's life! Fancy! I never saw a street for more than two years. Didn't you miss them in the war?

JOHNNY. I missed grass and trees more—the trees! All burnt, and splintered. Gah!

FAITH. Yes, I like trees too; anything beautiful, you know. I think the parks are lovely—but they might let you pick the flowers. But the lights are best, really—they make you feel happy. And music—I love an organ. There was one used to come and play outside the prison—before I was tried. It sounded so far away and lovely. If I could 'ave met the man that played that organ, I'd have kissed him. D'you think he did it on purpose?

JOHNNY. He would have, if he'd been me.

He says it unconsciously, but FAITH *is instantly conscious of the implication.*

FAITH. He'd rather have had pennies, though. It's all earning; working and earning. I wish I were like the flowers. [*She twirls the flower in her hand*] Flowers don't work, and they don't get put in prison.

JOHNNY. [*Putting his arm round her*] Never mind!

Cheer up! You're only a kid. You'll have a good time yet.

FAITH *leans against him, as it were indifferently, clearly expecting him to kiss her, but he doesn't.*

FAITH. When I was a little girl I had a cake covered with sugar. I ate the sugar all off and then I didn't want the cake—not much.

JOHNNY. [*Suddenly, removing his arm*] Gosh! If I could write a poem that would show everybody what was in the heart of everybody else——!

FAITH. It'd be too long for the papers, wouldn't it?

JOHNNY. It'd be too strong.

FAITH. Besides, you don't know. [*Her eyelids go up.*

JOHNNY. [*Staring at her*] I could tell what's in you now.

FAITH. What?

JOHNNY. You feel like a flower that's been picked.

[FAITH's *smile is enigmatic.*

FAITH. [*Suddenly*] Why do you go on about me so?

JOHNNY. Because you're weak—little and weak. [*Breaking out again*] Damn it! We went into the war to save the little and weak; at least we *said* so; and look at us now! The bottom's out of all that. [*Bitterly*] There isn't a faith or an illusion left. Look here! I want to help you.

FAITH. [*Surprisingly*] My baby was little and weak.

JOHNNY. You never meant—— You didn't do it for your own advantage.

FAITH. It didn't know it was alive. [*Suddenly*] D'you think I'm pretty?

JOHNNY. As pie.

FAITH. Then you'd better keep away, hadn't you?

JOHNNY. Why?

FAITH. You might want a bite.

JOHNNY. Oh! I can trust myself.

FAITH. [*Turning to the window, through which can be seen the darkening of a shower*] It's raining. Father says windows never stay clean.

They stand close together, unaware that COOK *has thrown up the service shutter, to see why the clearing takes so long. Her astounded head and shoulders pass into view just as* FAITH *suddenly puts up her face.* JOHNNY'S *lips hesitate, then move towards her forehead. But her face shifts, and they find themselves upon her lips. Once there, the emphasis cannot help but be considerable.* COOK'S *mouth falls open.*

COOK. Oh! [*She closes the shutter, vanishing.*

FAITH. What was that?

JOHNNY. Nothing. [*Breaking away*] Look here! I didn't mean—I oughtn't to have—— Please forget it!

FAITH. [*With a little smile*] Didn't you like it?

JOHNNY. Yes—that's just it. I didn't mean to—— It won't do.

FAITH. Why not?

JOHNNY. No, no! It's just the opposite of what—— No, no!

He goes to the door, wrenches it open and goes out.

FAITH, *still with that little half-mocking, half-contented smile, resumes the clearing of the table. She is interrupted by the entrance through the French windows of* MR. MARCH *and* MARY, *struggling with one small wet umbrella.*

MARY. [*Feeling his sleeve*] Go and change, Dad.

MR. MARCH. Women's shoes! We could have made the Tube but for your shoes.

MARY. It was *your* cold feet, not mine, dear. [*Looking at* FAITH *and nudging him*] Now!

She goes towards the door, turns to look at FAITH *still clearing the table, and goes out.*

MR. MARCH. [*In front of the hearth*] Nasty spring weather, Faith.

FAITH. [*Still in the mood of the kiss*] Yes, sir.

MR. MARCH. [*Sotto voce*] "In the spring a young man's fancy." I—I wanted to say something to you in a friendly way.

[FAITH *regards him as he struggles on.*

Because I feel very friendly towards you.

FAITH. Yes.

MR. MARCH. So you won't take what I say in bad part?

FAITH. No.

MR. MARCH. After what you've been through, any man with a sense of chivalry——

[FAITH *gives a little shrug.*

Yes, I know—but we don't all support the Government.

FAITH. I don't know anything about the Government.

MR. MARCH. [*Side-tracked on to his hobby*] Ah! I forgot. You saw no newspapers. But you ought to pick up the threads now. What paper does Cook take?

FAITH. "Cosy."

MR. MARCH. "Cosy"? I don't seem—— What are its politics?

FAITH. It hasn't any—only funny bits, and fashions. It's full of corsets.

MR. MARCH. What does Cook want with corsets?

FAITH. She likes to think she looks like that.

MR. MARCH. By George! Cook an idealist! Let's see!—er—I was speaking of chivalry. My son, you know—er—my son has got it.

FAITH. Badly?

MR. MARCH. [*Suddenly alive to the fact that she is playing with him*] I started by being sorry for *you*.

FAITH. Aren't you, any more?

MR. MARCH. Look here, my child!

[FAITH *looks up at him.*

[*Protectingly*] We want to do our best for you. Now, don't spoil it by—— Well, you know!

FAITH. [*Suddenly*] Suppose you'd been stuffed away in a hole for years!

MR. MARCH. [*Side-tracked again*] Just what your father said. The more I see of Mr. Bly, the more wise I think him.

FAITH. About other people.

MR. MARCH. What sort of bringing up did he give you?

[FAITH *smiles wryly and shrugs her shoulders.*

MR. MARCH. H'm! Here comes the sun again!

FAITH. [*Taking up the flower which is lying on the table*] May I have this flower?

MR. MARCH. Of course. You can always take what flowers you like—that is—if—er——

FAITH. If Mrs. March isn't about?

MR. MARCH. *I* meant, if it doesn't spoil the look of the table. We must all be artists in our professions, mustn't we?

FAITH. My profession was cutting hair. I *would* like to cut yours.

[MR. MARCH'S *hands instinctively go up to it.*

MR. MARCH. You mightn't think it, but I'm talking to you seriously.

FAITH. I was, too.

MR. MARCH. [*out of his depth*] Well! I got wet; I must go and change.

FAITH *follows him with her eyes as he goes out, and resumes the clearing of the table.*

She has paused and is again smelling at the flower when she hears the door, and quickly resumes her work. It is MRS. MARCH, *who comes in and goes to the writing table, Left Back, without looking at* FAITH. *She sits there writing a cheque, while* FAITH *goes on clearing.*

MRS. MARCH. [*Suddenly, in an unruffled voice*] I have made your cheque out for four pounds. It's rather more than the fortnight, and a month's notice. There'll be a cab for you in an hour's time. Can you be ready by then?

FAITH. [*Astonished*] What for—ma'am?

MRS. MARCH. You don't suit.

FAITH. Why?

MRS. MARCH. Do you wish for the reason?

FAITH. [*Breathless*] Yes.

MRS. MARCH. Cook saw you just now.

FAITH. [*Blankly*] Oh! I didn't mean her to.

MRS. MARCH. Obviously.

FAITH. I—I——

MRS. MARCH. Now go and pack up your things.

FAITH. He asked me to be a friend to him. He said he was lonely here.

MRS. MARCH. Don't be ridiculous. Cook saw you kissing him with p—p——

FAITH. [*Quickly*] *Not* with *pep*.

MRS. MARCH. I was going to say "passion." Now, go quietly.

FAITH. Where am I to go?

MRS. MARCH. You will have four pounds, and you can get another place.

FAITH. How?

MRS. MARCH. That's hardly my affair.

FAITH. [*Tossing her head*] All right!

MRS. MARCH. I'll speak to your father, if he isn't gone.

FAITH. Why do you send me away—just for a kiss! What's a kiss?

MRS. MARCH. That will do.

FAITH. [*Desperately*] He wanted to—to save me.

MRS. MARCH. You know perfectly well people can only save themselves.

FAITH. I don't care for your son; I've got a young —— [*She checks herself*] I—I'll leave your son alone; if he leave me.

[MRS. MARCH *rings the bell on the table.*

[*Desolately*] Well? [*She moves towards the door. Suddenly holding out the flower*] Mr. March gave me that flower; would you like it back?

MRS. MARCH. Don't be absurd! If you want more money till you get a place, let me know.

FAITH. I won't trouble you. [*She goes out.*

MRS. MARCH *goes to the window and drums her fingers on the pane.* COOK *enters.*

MRS. MARCH. Cook, if Mr. Bly's still here, I want to see him. Oh! And it's three now. Have a cab at four o'clock.

COOK. [*Almost tearful*] Oh, ma'am—anybody but Master Johnny, and I'd 'ave been a deaf an' dummy. Poor girl! She's not responsive, I daresay. Suppose I was to speak to Master Johnny?

MRS. MARCH. No, no, Cook! Where's Mr. Bly?

COOK. He's done his windows; he's just waiting for his money.

MRS. MARCH. Then get him; and take that tray.

COOK. I remember the master kissin' me, when he was a boy. But then he never meant anything; so different from Master Johnny. Master Johnny takes things to 'eart.

MRS. MARCH. Just so, Cook.

COOK. There's not an ounce of vice in 'im. It's all his goodness, dear little feller.

MRS. MARCH. That's the danger, with a girl like that.

COOK. It's eatin' hearty all of a sudden that's made her poptious. But there, ma'am, try her again. Master Johnny'll be so cut up!

MRS. MARCH. No playing with fire, Cook. We were foolish to let her come.

COOK. Oh! dear, he *will* be angry with me. If you hadn't been in the kitchen and heard me, ma'am, I'd ha' let it pass.

MRS. MARCH. That would have been very wrong of you.

COOK. Ah! But I'd do a lot of wrong things for Master Johnny. There's always some one you'll go wrong for!

MRS. MARCH. Well, get Mr. Bly; and take that tray, there's a good soul.

COOK *goes out with the tray; and while waiting,* MRS. MARCH *finishes clearing the table. She has not quite finished when* MR. BLY *enters.*

BLY. Your service, ma'am!

MRS. MARCH. [*With embarrassment*] I'm very sorry, Mr. Bly, but circumstances over which I have no control——

BLY. [*With deprecation*] Ah! we all has them. The winders *ought* to be done once a week now the Spring's on 'em.

MRS. MARCH. No, no; it's your daughter—

BLY. [*Deeply*] Not been givin' way to 'er instincts, I do trust.

MRS. MARCH. Yes. I've just had to say good-bye to her.

BLY. [*Very blank*] Nothing to do with property, I hope?

MRS. MARCH. No, no! Giddiness with my son. It's impossible; she really must learn.

BLY. Oh! but 'oo's to learn her? Couldn't you learn your son instead?

MRS. MARCH. No. My son is very high-minded.

BLY. [*Dubiously*] I see. How am I goin' to get over this? Shall I tell you what I think, ma'am?

MRS. MARCH. I'm afraid it'll be no good.

BLY. That's it. Character's born, not made. You can clean yer winders and clean 'em, but that don't change the colour of the glass. My father would have given her a good hidin', but I shan't. Why not? Because my glass ain't as thick as his. I see through it; I see my girl's temptations, I see what she is—likes a bit o' life, likes a flower, an' a dance. She's a natural morganatic.

MRS. MARCH. A what?

BLY. Nothin'll ever make her regular. Mr. March'll understand how I feel. Poor girl! In the mud again. Well, we must keep smilin'. [*His face is as long as his arm*] The poor 'ave their troubles, there's no doubt. [*He turns to go*] There's nothin' can save her but money, so as she can do as she likes. Then she wouldn't want to do it.

MRS. MARCH. I'm very sorry, but there it is.

BLY. And I thought she was goin' to be a success here. Fact is, you can't see anything till it 'appens. There's winders all round, but you can't see. Follow your instincts—it's the only way.

MRS. MARCH. It hasn't helped your daughter.

BLY. I was speakin' philosophic! Well, I'll go 'ome now, and prepare meself for the worst.

MRS. MARCH. Has Cook given you your money?

BLY. She 'as.

He goes out gloomily and is nearly overthrown in the doorway by the violent entry of JOHNNY.

JOHNNY. What's this, Mother? I won't have it—it's pre-war.

MRS. MARCH. [*Indicating* MR. BLY] Johnny!

JOHNNY *waves* BLY *out of the room and closes the door.*

JOHNNY. I won't have her go. She's a pathetic little creature.

MRS. MARCH. [*Unruffled*] She's a minx.

JOHNNY. Mother!

MRS. MARCH. Now, Johnny, be sensible. She's a very pretty girl, and this is my house.

JOHNNY. Of course you think the worst. Trust anyone who wasn't in the war for that!

MRS. MARCH. I don't think either the better or the worse. Kisses are kisses!

JOHNNY. Mother, you're like the papers—you put in all the vice and leave out all the virtue, and call that human nature. The kiss was an accident that I bitterly regret.

MRS. MARCH. Johnny, how can you?

JOHNNY. Dash it! You know what I mean. I regret it with my—my conscience. It shan't occur again.

MRS. MARCH. Till next time.

JOHNNY. Mother, you make me despair. You're so matter-of-fact, you never give one credit for a pure ideal.

MRS. MARCH. I know where ideals lead.

JOHNNY. Where?

MRS. MARCH. Into the soup. And the purer they are, the hotter the soup.

JOHNNY. And you married father!

MRS. MARCH. I did.

JOHNNY. Well, that girl is not to be chucked out; I won't have her on my chest.

MRS. MARCH. That's why she's going, Johnny.

JOHNNY. She is not. Look at me!

> MRS. MARCH *looks at him from across the dining-table, for he has marched up to it, till they are staring at each other across the now cleared rosewood.*

MRS. MARCH. How are you going to stop her?

JOHNNY. Oh, I'll stop her right enough. If I stuck it out in Hell, I can stick it out in Highgate.

MRS. MARCH. Johnny, listen. I've watched this girl; and I don't watch what I want to see—like your father—I watch what *is*. She's not a hard case—yet; but she will be.

JOHNNY. And why? Because all you matter-of-fact

people make up your minds to it. What earthly chance has she had?

MRS. MARCH. She's a baggage. There are such things, you know, Johnny.

JOHNNY. She's a little creature who went down in the scrum and has been kicked about ever since.

MRS. MARCH. I'll give her money, if you'll keep her at arm's length.

JOHNNY. I call that revolting. What she wants is the human touch.

MRS. MARCH. I've not a doubt of it.

[JOHNNY *rises in disgust.*

Johnny, what is the use of wrapping the thing up in catchwords? Human touch! A young man like you never saved a girl like her. It's as fantastic as—as Tolstoi's "Resurrection."

JOHNNY. Tolstoi was the most truthful writer that ever lived.

MRS. MARCH. Tolstoi was a Russian—always proving that what isn't, is.

JOHNNY. Russians are charitable, anyway, and see into other people's souls.

MRS. MARCH. That's why they're hopeless.

JOHNNY. Well—for cynicism——

MRS. MARCH. It's at least as important, Johnny, to see into ourselves as into other people. I've been trying to make your father understand that ever since we married. He'd be such a good writer if he did—he wouldn't write at all.

JOHNNY. Father has imagination.

MRS. MARCH. And no business to meddle with practical affairs. You and he always ride in front of the hounds. Do you remember when the war broke out, how angry you were with me because I said we were fighting from a sense of self-preservation? Well, weren't we?

JOHNNY. That's what I'm doing now, anyway.

MRS. MARCH. Saving this girl, to save yourself?

JOHNNY. I must have something decent to do sometimes. There isn't an ideal left.

MRS. MARCH. If you knew how tired I am of the word, Johnny!

JOHNNY. There are thousands who feel like me—that the bottom's out of everything. It sickens me that anything in the least generous should get sat on by all you people who haven't risked your lives.

MRS. MARCH. [*With a smile*] I risked mine when you were born, Johnny. You were always very difficult.

JOHNNY. That girl's been telling me—I can see the whole thing.

MRS. MARCH. The fact that she suffered doesn't alter her nature; or the danger to you and us.

JOHNNY. There *is* no danger—I told her I didn't mean it.

MRS. MARCH. And she smiled? Didn't she?

JOHNNY. I—I don't know.

MRS. MARCH. If you were ordinary, Johnny, it would be the girl's look-out. But you're not, and I'm not going to have you in the trap she'll set for you.

JOHNNY. You think she's a designing minx. I tell

you she's got no more design in her than a rabbit. She's just at the mercy of anything.

MRS. MARCH. That's the trap. She'll play on your feelings, and you'll be caught.

JOHNNY. I'm not a baby.

MRS. MARCH. You are—and she'll smother *you*.

JOHNNY. How beastly women are to each other!

MRS. MARCH. We know ourselves, you see. The girl's father realises perfectly what she is.

JOHNNY. Mr. Bly is a dodderer. And she's got no mother. I'll bet you've never realised the life girls who get outed lead. I've seen them—I saw them in France. It gives one the horrors.

MRS. MARCH. I can imagine it. But no girl gets "outed," as you call it, unless she's predisposed that way.

JOHNNY. That's all you know of the pressure of life.

MRS. MARCH. Excuse me, Johnny. I worked three years among factory girls, and I know how they manage to resist things when they've got stuff in them.

JOHNNY. Yes, I know what you mean by stuff—good hard self-preservative instinct. Why should the wretched girl who hasn't got that be turned down? She wants protection all the more.

MRS. MARCH. I've offered to help with money till she gets a place.

JOHNNY. And you know she won't take it. She's got that much stuff in her. This place is her only chance. I appeal to you, Mother—please tell her not to go.

Mrs. March. I shall not, Johnny.

Johnny. [*Turning abruptly*] Then we know where we are.

Mrs. March. I know where you'll be before a week's over.

Johnny. Where?

Mrs. March. In her arms.

Johnny. [*From the door, grimly*] If I am, I'll have the right to be!

Mrs. March. Johnny! [*But he is gone.*

Mrs. March *follows to call him back, but is met by* Mary.

Mary. So you've tumbled, Mother?

Mrs. March. I should think I have! Johnny is making an idiot of himself about that girl.

Mary. He's got the best intentions.

Mrs. March. It's all your father. What can one expect when your father carries on like a lunatic over his paper every morning?

Mary. Father must have opinions of his own.

Mrs. March. He has only one: Whatever is, is wrong.

Mary. He can't help being intellectual, Mother.

Mrs. March. If he would only learn that the value of a sentiment is the amount of sacrifice you are prepared to make for it!

Mary. Yes: I read that in "The Times" yesterday. Father's much safer than Johnny. Johnny isn't safe at all; he might make a sacrifice any day. What were they doing?

MRS. MARCH. Cook caught them kissing.

MARY. How truly horrible!

[*As she speaks* MR. MARCH *comes in.*

MR. MARCH. I met Johnny using the most poetic language. What's happened?

MRS. MARCH. He and that girl. Johnny's talking nonsense about wanting to save her. I've told her to pack up.

MR. MARCH. Isn't that rather coercive, Joan?

MRS. MARCH. Do you approve of Johnny getting entangled with this girl?

MR. MARCH. No. I was only saying to Mary——

MRS. MARCH. Oh! You were!

MR. MARCH. But I can quite see why Johnny——

MRS. MARCH. The Government, I suppose!

MR. MARCH. Certainly.

MRS. MARCH. Well, perhaps you'll get us out of the mess you've got us into.

MR. MARCH. Where's the girl?

MRS. MARCH. In her room—packing.

MR. MARCH. We must devise means—

[MRS. MARCH *smiles.*

The first thing is to see into them—and find out exactly——

MRS. MARCH. Heavens! Are you going to have them X-rayed? They haven't got chest trouble, Geof.

MR. MARCH. They may have heart trouble. It's no good being hasty, Joan.

MRS. MARCH. Oh! For a man that can't see an inch into human nature, give me a—psychological novelist!

Mr. March. [*With dignity*] Mary, go and see where Johnny is.

Mary. Do you want him here?

Mr. March. Yes.

Mary. [*Dubiously*] Well—if I can. [*She goes out. A silence, during which the* Marches *look at each other by those turns which characterise exasperated domesticity.*

Mrs. March. If she doesn't go, Johnny must. Are you going to turn him out?

Mr. March. Of course not. We must reason with him.

Mrs. March. Reason with young people whose lips were glued together half an hour ago! Why ever did you force me to take this girl?

Mr. March. [*Ruefully*] One can't *always* resist a kindly impulse, Joan. What does Mr. Bly say to it?

Mrs. March. Mr. Bly? "Follow your instincts"—and then complains of his daughter for following them.

Mr. March. The man's a philosopher.

Mrs. March. Before we know where we are, we shall be having Johnny married to that girl.

Mr. March. Nonsense!

Mrs. March. Oh, Geof! Whenever you're faced with reality, you say "Nonsense!" You know Johnny's got chivalry on the brain.

[Mary *comes in.*

Mary. He's at the top of the servant's staircase, outside her room. He's sitting in an armchair, with its back to her door.

MR. MARCH. Good Lord! Direct action!

MARY. He's got his pipe, a pound of chocolate, three volumes of "Monte Cristo," and his old concertina. He says it's better than the trenches.

MR. MARCH. My hat! Johnny's made a joke. This is serious.

MARY. Nobody can get up, and she can't get down. He says he'll stay there till all's blue, and it's no use either of you coming unless mother caves in.

MR. MARCH. I wonder if Cook could do anything with him?

MARY. She's tried. He told her to go to hell.

MR. MARCH. I say! And what did Cook——?

MARY. She's gone.

MR. MARCH. Tt! tt! This is very awkward.

COOK *enters through the door which* MARY *has left open.*

MR. MARCH. Ah, Cook! You're back, then? What's to be done?

MRS. MARCH. [*With a laugh*] We must devise means!

COOK. Oh, ma'am, it does remind me so of the tantrums he used to get into, dear little feller!

[*Smiles with recollection.*

MRS. MARCH. [*Sharply*] You're not to take him up anything to eat, Cook!

COOK. Oh! But Master Johnny does get so hungry. It'll drive him wild, ma'am. Just a snack now and then!

MRS. MARCH. No, Cook. Mind—that's flat!

COOK. Aren't I to feed Faith, ma'am?

MR. MARCH. Gad! It wants it!

MRS. MARCH. Johnny must come down to earth.

COOK. Ah! I remember how he used to fall down when he was little—he *would* go about with his head in the air. But he always picked himself up like a little man.

MARY. Listen!

They all listen. The distant sounds of a concertina being played with fury drift in through the open door.

COOK. Don't it sound *'eavenly!*

[*The concertina utters a long wail.*

CURTAIN.

ACT III

ACT III

The March's *dining-room on the same evening at the end of a perfunctory dinner.* Mrs. March *sits at the dining-table with her back to the windows,* Mary *opposite the hearth, and* Mr. March *with his back to it.* Johnny *is not present. Silence and gloom.*

Mr. March. We always seem to be eating.

Mrs. March. *You've* eaten nothing.

Mr. March. [*Pouring himself out a liqueur glass of brandy but not drinking it*] It's humiliating to think we can't exist without. [*Relapses into gloom.*

Mrs. March. Mary, pass him the walnuts.

Mary. I was thinking of taking them up to Johnny.

Mr. March. [*Looking at his watch*] He's been there six hours; even he can't live on faith.

Mrs. March. If Johnny wants to make a martyr of himself, I can't help it.

Mary. How many days are you going to let him sit up there, Mother?

Mr. March. [*Glancing at* Mrs. March] I never in my life knew anything so ridiculous.

Mrs. March. Give me a little glass of brandy, Geof.

Mr. March. Good! That's the first step towards seeing reason.

He pours brandy into a liqueur glass from the decanter which stands between them. MRS. MARCH *puts the brandy to her lips and makes a little face, then swallows it down manfully.* MARY *gets up with the walnuts and goes. Silence. Gloom.*

MRS. MARCH. Horrid stuff!

MR. MARCH. Haven't you begun to see that your policy's hopeless, Joan? Come! Tell the girl she can stay. If we make Johnny *feel* victorious—we can deal with him. It's just personal pride—the curse of this world. Both you and Johnny are as stubborn as mules.

MRS. MARCH. Human nature *is* stubborn, Geof. That's what you easy-going people never see.

MR. MARCH *gets up, vexed, and goes to the fireplace.*

MR. MARCH. [*Turning*] Well! This goes further than you think. It involves Johnny's affection and respect for you.

MRS. MARCH *nervously refills the little brandy glass, and again empties it, with a grimacing shudder.*

MR. MARCH. [*Noticing*] That's better! You'll begin to see things presently.

[MARY *re-enters.*

MARY. He's been digging himself in. He's put a screen across the head of the stairs, and got Cook's blankets. He's going to sleep there.

MRS. MARCH. Did he take the walnuts?

MARY. No; he passed them in to *her*. He says he's on hunger strike. But he's eaten all the chocolate and smoked himself sick. He's having the time of his life, Mother.

MR. MARCH. There you are!

MRS. MARCH. Wait till this time to-morrow.

MARY. Cook's been up again. He wouldn't let her pass. She'll have to sleep in the spare room.

MR. MARCH. I say!

MARY. And he's got the books out of her room.

MRS. MARCH. D'you know what they are? "The Scarlet Pimpernel," "The Wide Wide World," and the Bible.

MARY. Johnny likes romance. [*She crosses to the fire.*

MR. MARCH. [*In a low voice*] Are you going to leave him up there with the girl and that inflammatory literature, all night? Where's your common sense, Joan?

MRS. MARCH *starts up, presses her hand over her brow, and sits down again. She is stumped.*

[*With consideration for her defeat*] Have another tot! [*He pours it out*] Let Mary go up with a flag of truce, and ask them both to come down for a thorough discussion of the whole thing, on condition that they can go up again if we don't come to terms.

MRS. MARCH. Very well! I'm quite willing to meet him. I hate quarrelling with Johnny.

MR. MARCH. Good! I'll go myself. [*He goes out.*

MARY. Mother, this isn't a coal strike; *don't* discuss it for three hours and then at the end ask Johnny and the girl to do precisely what you're asking them to do now!

MRS. MARCH. Why should I?

MARY. Because it's so usual. Do fix on half-way at once.

MRS. MARCH. There is no half-way.

MARY. Well, for goodness sake think of a plan which will make you both *look* victorious. That's always done in the end. Why not let her stay, and make Johnny promise only to see her in the presence of a third party?

MRS. MARCH. Because she'd see him every day while he was looking for the third party. She'd help him look for it.

MARY. [*With a gurgle*] Mother, I'd no idea you were so—French.

MRS. MARCH. It seems to me you none of you have any idea what I am.

MARY. Well, do remember that there'll be no publicity to make either of you look small. You can have Peace with Honour, whatever you decide. [*Listening*] There they are! Now, Mother, don't be logical! It's so *feminine.*

As the door opens, MRS. MARCH *nervously fortifies herself with the third little glass of brandy. She remains seated.* MARY *is on her right.*

MR. MARCH *leads into the room and stands next his daughter, then* FAITH *in hat and coat to the left of the table, and* JOHNNY, *pale but determined, last. Assembled thus, in a half fan, of which* MRS. MARCH *is the apex, so to speak, they are all extremely embarrassed, and no wonder.*

[*Suddenly* MARY *gives a little gurgle.*

JOHNNY. You'd think it funnier if you'd just come out of prison and were going to be chucked out of your job, on to the world again.

FAITH. I didn't want to come down here. If I'm to go I want to go at once. And if I'm not, it's my evening out, please.

She moves towards the door. JOHNNY *takes her by the shoulders.*

JOHNNY. Stand still, and leave it to me. [FAITH *looks up at him, hypnotized by his determination*] Now, mother, I've come down at your request to discuss this; are you ready to keep her? Otherwise up we go again.

MR. MARCH. That's not the way to go to work, Johnny. You mustn't ask people to eat their words raw—like that.

JOHNNY. Well, I've had no dinner, but I'm not going to eat *my* words, I tell you plainly.

MRS. MARCH. Very well then; go up again.

MARY. [*Muttering*] Mother—logic.

MR. MARCH. Great Scott! You two haven't the faintest idea of how to conduct a parley. We have—to—er—explore every path to find a way to peace.

MRS. MARCH. [*To* FAITH] Have you thought of anything to do, if you leave here?

FAITH. Yes.

JOHNNY. What?

FAITH. I shan't say.

JOHNNY. Of course, she'll just chuck herself away.

FAITH. No, I won't. I'll go to a place I know of, where they don't want references.

JOHNNY. Exactly!

MRS. MARCH. [*To* FAITH] I want to ask you a question. Since you came out, is this the first young man who's kissed you?

FAITH *has hardly had time to start and manifest what may or may not be indignation when* MR. MARCH *dashes his hands through his hair.*

MR. MARCH. Joan, really!

JOHNNY. [*Grimly*] Don't condescend to answer!

MRS. MARCH. I thought we'd met to get at the truth.

MARY. But do they ever?

FAITH. I *will* go out!

JOHNNY. No! [*And, as his back is against the door, she can't*] *I'll* see that you're not insulted any more.

MR. MARCH. Johnny, I know you have the best intentions, but really the proper people to help the young are the old—like——

FAITH *suddenly turns her eyes on him, and he goes on rather hurriedly*

—your mother. I'm sure that she and I will be ready to stand by Faith.

FAITH. I don't want charity.

MR. MARCH. No, no! But I hope——

MRS. MARCH. To devise means.

MR. MARCH. [*Roused*] Of course, if nobody will modify their attitude—Johnny, you ought to be ashamed of yourself, and [*To* MRS. MARCH] so ought you, Joan.

JOHNNY. [*Suddenly*] I'll modify mine. [*To* FAITH] Come here—close! [*In a low voice to* FAITH] Will you give me your word to stay here, if I make them keep you?

FAITH. Why?

JOHNNY. To stay here quietly for the next two years?

FAITH. I don't know.

JOHNNY. I can make them, if you'll promise.

FAITH. You're just in a temper.

JOHNNY. Promise!

During this colloquy the MARCHES *have been so profoundly uneasy that* MRS. MARCH *has poured out another glass of brandy.*

MR. MARCH. Johnny, the terms of the Armistice didn't include this sort of thing. It was to be all open and above-board.

JOHNNY. Well, if you don't keep her, I shall clear out. [*At this bombshell* MRS. MARCH *rises.*

MARY. Don't joke, Johnny! You'll do yourself an injury.

JOHNNY. And if I go, I go for good.

MR. MARCH. Nonsense, Johnny! Don't carry a good thing too far!

JOHNNY. I mean it.

MRS. MARCH. What will you live on?

JOHNNY. Not poetry.

MRS. MARCH. What, then?

JOHNNY. Emigrate or go into the Police.

MR. MARCH. Good Lord! [*Going up to his wife—in a low voice*] Let her stay till Johnny's in his right mind.

FAITH. I don't want to stay.

JOHNNY. You shall!

MARY. Johnny, don't be a lunatic!

[COOK *enters, flustered.*

COOK. Mr. Bly, ma'am, come after his daughter.

MR. MARCH. He can have her—he can have her!

COOK. Yes, sir. But, you see, he's—— Well, there! He's cheerful.

MR. MARCH. Let him come and take his daughter away.

But MR. BLY *has entered behind him. He has a fixed expression, and speaks with a too perfect accuracy.*

BLY. Did your two Cooks tell you I'm here?

MR. MARCH. If you want your daughter, you can take her.

JOHNNY. Mr. Bly, get out!

BLY. [*Ignoring him*] I don't want any fuss with your two cooks. [*Catching sight of* MRS. MARCH] I've prepared myself for this.

MRS. MARCH. So we see.

BLY. I 'ad a bit o' trouble, but I kep' on till I see 'Aigel walkin' at me in the loo-lookin' glass. Then I knew I'd got me balance.

They all regard MR. BLY *in a fascinated manner.*

FAITH. Father! You've been drinking.

BLY. [*Smiling*] What do you think?

MR. MARCH. We have a certain sympathy with you, Mr. Bly.

BLY. [*Gazing at his daughter*] I don't want that one. I'll take the other.

MARY. Don't repeat yourself, Mr. Bly.

BLY. [*With a flash of muddled insight*] *Well!* There's two of everybody; two of my daughter; an' two of the 'Ome Secretary; and two—two of Cook—an' I don't want either. [*He waves* COOK *aside, and grasps at a void alongside* FAITH] Come along!

MR. MARCH. [*Going up to him*] Very well, Mr. Bly! See her home, carefully. Good-night!

BLY Shake hands!

He extends his other hand; MR. MARCH *grasps it and turns him round towards the door.*

MR. MARCH. Now, take her away! Cook, go and open the front door for Mr. Bly and his daughter.

BLY. Too many Cooks!

MR. MARCH. Now then, Mr. Bly, take her along!

BLY. [*Making no attempt to acquire the real* FAITH—*to an apparition which he leads with his right hand*] You're the one that died when my girl was 'ung. Will you go first or shall—I?

[*The apparition does not answer.*

MARY. Don't! It's horrible!

FAITH. I *did* die.

BLY. Prepare yourself. Then you'll see what you never saw before.

He goes out with his apparition, shepherded by MR. MARCH.

MRS. MARCH *drinks off her fourth glass of brandy. A peculiar whistle is heard through the open door, and* FAITH *starts forward.*

JOHNNY. Stand still!

FAITH. I—I must go.

MARY. Johnny—let her!

FAITH. There's a friend waiting for me.

JOHNNY. Let her wait! You're not fit to go out to-night.

MARY. Johnny! Really! You're not the girl's Friendly Society!

JOHNNY. You none of you care a pin's head what becomes of her. Can't you see she's on the edge.

[*The whistle is heard again, but fainter.*

FAITH. I'm not in prison now.

JOHNNY. [*Taking her by the arm*] All right! I'll come with you.

FAITH. [*Recoiling*] No. [*Voices are heard in the hall.*

MARY. Who's that with father? Johnny, for goodness' sake don't make us all ridiculous.

MR. MARCH'S *voice is heard saying: "Your friend is in here." He enters, followed by a reluctant young man in a dark suit, with dark hair and a pale square face, enlivened by strange, very living, dark, bull's eyes.*

MR. MARCH. [*To* FAITH, *who stands shrinking a little*] I came on this—er—friend of yours outside; he's been waiting for you some time, he says.

MRS. MARCH. [*To* FAITH] You can go now.

JOHNNY [*Suddenly, to the* YOUNG MAN] Who are you?

YOUNG M. Ask another! [*To* FAITH] Are you ready?

JOHNNY. [*Seeing red*] No, she's not; and you'll just clear out.

MR. MARCH. Johnny!

YOUNG M. What have *you* got to do with her?

JOHNNY. Quit.

YOUNG M. I'll quit with her, and not before. She's my girl.

JOHNNY. *Are* you his girl?

FAITH. Yes.

MRS. MARCH *sits down again, and reaching out her left hand, mechanically draws to her the glass of brandy which her husband had poured out for himself and left undrunk.*

JOHNNY. Then why did you— [*He is going to say: "Kiss me," but checks himself*]—let me think you hadn't any friends? Who is this fellow?

YOUNG M. A little more civility, please.

JOHNNY. You look a blackguard, and I believe you are.

MR. MARCH. [*With perfunctory authority*] I really can't have this sort of thing in my house. Johnny, go upstairs; and you two, please go away.

YOUNG M. [*To* JOHNNY] We know the sort of chap *you* are—takin' advantage of workin' girls.

JOHNNY. That's a foul lie. Come into the garden and I'll prove it on your carcase.

YOUNG M. All right!

FAITH. No; he'll hurt you. He's been in the war.

JOHNNY. [*To the* YOUNG MAN] *You* haven't, I'll bet.

YOUNG M. I didn't come here to be slanged.

JOHNNY. This poor girl is going to have a fair deal, and *you're* not going to give it her. I can see that with half an eye.

YOUNG M. You'll see it with no eyes when I've done with you.

JOHNNY. Come on, then. [*He goes up to the windows.*

MR. MARCH. For God's sake, Johnny, stop this vulgar brawl!

FAITH. [*Suddenly*] I'm not a "poor girl" and I won't be called one. I don't want any soft words. Why can't you let me be? [*Pointing to* JOHNNY] He talks wild. [JOHNNY *clutches the edge of the writing-table*] Thinks he can "rescue" me. I don't want to be rescued. I— [*All the feeling of years rises to the surface now that the barrier has broken*] I want to be let alone. I've paid for everything I've done—a pound for every shilling's worth. And all because of one minute when I was half crazy. [*Flashing round at* MARY] Wait till *you've* had a baby you oughtn't to have had, and not a penny in your pocket! It's money—money—all money!

YOUNG M. Sst! That'll do!

FAITH. I'll have what I like now, not what you think's good for me.

MR. MARCH. God knows we don't want to——

FAITH. You mean very well, Mr. March, but you're no good.

MR. MARCH. I knew it.

FAITH. You were very kind to me. But you don't see; nobody *sees*.

YOUNG M. There! That's enough! You're gettin' excited. You come away with me.

FAITH'S *look at him is like the look of a dog at her master.*

JOHNNY. [*From the background*] I know you're a blackguard—I've seen your sort.

FAITH. [*Firing up*] Don't call him names! I won't have it. I'll go with whom I choose! [*Her eyes suddenly fix themselves on the* YOUNG MAN'S *face*] And I'm going with him!

[COOK *enters.*

MR. MARCH. What now, Cook?

COOK. A Mr. Barnabas in the hall, sir. From the police.

Everybody starts. MRS. MARCH *drinks off her fifth little glass of brandy, then sits again.*

MR. MARCH. From the police?

He goes out, followed by COOK. *A moment's suspense.*

YOUNG M. Well, I can't wait any longer. I suppose we can go out the back way?

He draws FAITH *towards the windows. But* JOHNNY *stands there, barring the way.*

JOHNNY. No, you don't.

FAITH. [*Scared*] Oh! Let me go—let him go!

JOHNNY. *You* may go. [*He takes her arm to pull her to the window*] He can't.

FAITH. [*Freeing herself*] No—no! Not if he doesn't.

JOHNNY *has an evident moment of hesitation, and before it is over* MR. MARCH *comes in again, followed by a man in a neat suit of plain clothes.*

MR. MARCH. I should like you to say that in front of her.

P. C. MAN. Your service, ma'am. Afraid I'm intruding here. Fact is, I've been waiting for a chance to speak to this young woman quietly. It's rather public here, sir; but if you wish, of course, I'll mention it. [*He waits for some word from some one; no one speaks, so he goes on almost apologetically*] Well, now, you're in a good place here, and you ought to keep it. You don't want fresh trouble, I'm sure.

FAITH. [*Scared*] What do you want with me?

P. C. MAN. I don't want to frighten you; but we've had word passed that you're associating with the young man there. I observed him to-night again, waiting outside here and whistling.

YOUNG M. What's the matter with whistling?

P. C. MAN. [*Eyeing him*] I should keep quiet if I was you. As *you* know, sir [*To* MR. MARCH] there's a law nowadays against soo-tenors.

MR. MARCH. Soo——?

JOHNNY. I knew it.

P. C. MAN. [*Deprecating*] I don't want to use any plain English—with ladies present——

YOUNG M. I don't know you. What are you after? Do you dare——?

P. C. MAN. We cut the darin', 'tisn't necessary. We know all about you.

FAITH. It's a lie!

P. C. MAN. There, miss, don't let your feelings——

FAITH. [*To the* YOUNG MAN] It's a lie, isn't it?

YOUNG M. A blankety lie.

MR. MARCH. [*To* BARNABAS] Have you actual proof?

YOUNG M. Proof? It's his job to get chaps into a mess.

P. C. MAN. [*Sharply*] None of your lip, now!

At the new tone in his voice FAITH *turns and visibly quails, like a dog that has been shown a whip.*

MR. MARCH. Inexpressibly painful!

YOUNG M. Ah! How would you like to be insulted in front of your girl? If you're a gentleman you'll tell him to leave the house. If he's got a warrant, let him produce it; if he hasn't, let him get out.

P. C. MAN. [*To* MR. MARCH] You'll understand, sir, that my object in speakin' to you to-night was for the good of the girl. Strictly, I've gone a bit out of my way. If my job was to get men into trouble, as he says, I'd only to wait till he's got hold of her. These fellows, you know, are as cunning as lynxes and as impudent as the devil.

YOUNG M. Now, look here, if I get any more of this from you—I—I'll consult a lawyer.

JOHNNY. Fellows like you——

MR. MARCH. Johnny!

P. C. MAN. Your son, sir?

YOUNG M. Yes; and wants to be where I am. But my girl knows better; don't you?

He gives FAITH *a look which has a certain magnetism.*

P. C. MAN. If we could have the Court cleared of ladies, sir, we might speak a little plainer.

MR. MARCH. Joan!

But MRS. MARCH *does not vary her smiling immobility;* FAITH *draws a little nearer to the* YOUNG MAN. MARY *turns to the fire.*

P. C. MAN. [*With half a smile*] I keep on forgettin' that women are men nowadays. Well!

YOUNG M. When you've quite done joking, we'll go for our walk.

MR. MARCH. [*To* BARNABAS] I think you'd better tell her anything you know.

P. C. MAN. [*Eyeing* FAITH *and the* YOUNG MAN] I'd rather not be more precise, sir, at this stage.

YOUNG M. I should think not! Police spite! [*To* FAITH] *You* know what the Law is, once they get a down on you.

P. C. MAN. [*To* MR. MARCH] It's our business to keep an eye on all this sort of thing, sir, with girls who've just come out.

JOHNNY. [*Deeply*] You've only to look at his face!

YOUNG M. My face is as good as yours.

[FAITH *lifts her eyes to his.*

P. C. MAN. [*Taking in that look*] Well, there it is! Sorry I wasted my time and yours, sir!

MR. MARCH. [*Distracted*] My goodness! Now,

Faith, consider! This is the turning-point. I've told you we'll stand by you.

FAITH. [*Flashing round*] Leave me alone! I stick to my friends. Leave me alone, and leave him alone! What is it to you?

P. C. MAN. [*With sudden resolution*] Now, look here! This man George Blunter was had up three years ago for livin' on the earnings of a woman called Johnson. He was dismissed with a caution. We got him again last year over a woman called Lee—that time he did——

YOUNG M. Stop it! That's enough of your lip. I won't put up with this—not for any woman in the world. Not I!

FAITH. [*With a sway towards him*] It's not——!

YOUNG M. I'm off! Bong Swore la Companee!

He turns on his heel and walks out unhindered.

P. C. MAN. [*Deeply*] A bad hat, that; if ever there was one. We'll be having him again before long.

He looks at FAITH. *They all look at* FAITH. *But her face is so strange, so tremulous, that they all turn their eyes away.*

FAITH. He—he said—he——!

On the verge of an emotional outbreak, she saves herself by an effort. A painful silence.

P. C. MAN. Well, sir—that's all. Good evening!

He turns to the door, touching his forehead to MR. MARCH, *and goes.*

As the door closes, FAITH *sinks into a chair, and burying her face in her hands, sobs silently.* MRS. MARCH *sits motionless with a faint smile.* JOHNNY *stands at the window biting his nails.* MARY *crosses to* FAITH.

MARY. [*Softly*] Don't. You weren't really fond of him?

[FAITH *bends her head.*

MARY. But how could you? He——!

FAITH. I—I couldn't see inside him.

MARY. Yes; but he looked—couldn't you see he looked——?

FAITH. [*Suddenly flinging up her head*] If you'd been two years without a word, you'd believe anyone that said he liked you.

MARY. Perhaps I should.

FAITH. But I don't want him—he's a liar. I don't like liars.

MARY. I'm awfully sorry.

FAITH. [*Looking at her*] Yes—you keep off feeling—then you'll be happy! [*Rising*] Good-bye!

MARY. Where are you going?

FAITH. To my father.

MARY. With him in that state?

FAITH. *He* won't hurt me.

MARY. You'd better stay. Mother, she *can* stay, can't she?

[MRS. MARCH *nods.*

FAITH. No!

MARY. Why not? We're all sorry. Do! You'd better.

FAITH. Father'll come over for my things to-morrow.

MARY. What are you going to do?

FAITH. [*Proudly*] I'll get on.

JOHNNY. [*From the window*] Stop!

[*All turn and look at him. He comes down.*

Will you come to *me?*

FAITH *stares at him.* MRS. MARCH *continues to smile faintly.*

MARY. [*With a horrified gesture*] Johnny!

JOHNNY. Will you? I'll play cricket if you do.

MR. MARCH. [*Under his breath*] Good God!

He stares in suspense at FAITH, *whose face is a curious blend of fascination and live feeling.*

JOHNNY. Well?

FAITH. [*Softly*] Don't be silly! I've got no call on you. You don't care for me, and I don't for you. No! You go and put your head in ice. [*She turns to the door*] Good-bye, Mr. March! I'm sorry I've been so much trouble.

MR. MARCH. Not at all, not at all!

FAITH. Oh! Yes, I have. There's nothing to be done with a girl like me. [*She goes out.*

JOHNNY. [*Taking up the decanter to pour himself out a glass of brandy*] Empty!

COOK. [*Who has entered with a tray*] Yes, my dearie, I'm sure you are.

JOHNNY. [*Staring at his father*] A vision, Dad! Windows of Clubs—men sitting there; and that girl going by with rouge on her cheeks——

COOK. Oh! Master Johnny!

JOHNNY. A blue night—the moon over the Park.

And she stops and looks at it.—— What has she wanted—the beautiful—something better than she's got—something that she'll never get!

COOK. Oh! Master Johnny!

She goes up to JOHNNY *and touches his forehead. He comes to himself and hurries to the door, but suddenly* MRS. MARCH *utters a little feathery laugh. She stands up, swaying slightly. There is something unusual and charming in her appearance, as if formality had dropped from her.*

MRS. MARCH. [*With a sort of delicate slow lack of perfect sobriety*] I see—it—all. You—can't—help—unless—you—love!

[JOHNNY *stops and looks round at her.*

MR. MARCH. [*Moving a little towards her*] Joan!

MRS. MARCH. She—wants—to—be—loved. It's the way of the world.

MARY. [*Turning*] Mother!

MRS. MARCH. You thought she wanted—to be saved. Silly! She — just — wants — to — be — loved. Quite natural!

MR. MARCH. Joan, what's happened to you?

MRS. MARCH. [*Smiling and nodding*] See—people—as—they—are! Then you won't be—disappointed. Don't—have—ideals! Have—vision—just simple—vision!

MR. MARCH. Your mother's not well.

MRS. MARCH. [*Passing her hand over her forehead*] It's hot in here!

MR. MARCH. Mary!

[MARY *throws open the French windows.*

MRS. MARCH. [*Delightfully*] The room's full of—GAS. Open the windows! Open! And let's—walk—out—into the air!

She turns and walks delicately out through the opened windows; JOHNNY *and* MARY *follow her. The moonlight and the air flood in.*

COOK. [*Coming to the table and taking up the empty decanter*] My Holy Ma!

MR. MARCH. Is this the Millennium, Cook?

COOK. Oh! Master Geoffrey—there isn't a millehennium. There's too much human nature. We must look things in the face.

MR. MARCH. Ah! Neither up—nor down—but straight in the face! Quite a thought, Cook! Quite a thought!

CURTAIN.